T0380597

FADING
MEMORIES

MS. JOYCE SMITH

WESTBOW
PRESS®
A DIVISION OF THOMAS NELSON
& ZONDERVAN

Copyright © 2020 Ms. Joyce Smith.

All rights reserved. No part of this book may be used or reproduced by any means,
graphic, electronic, or mechanical, including photocopying, recording, taping or by
any information storage retrieval system without the written permission of the author
except in the case of brief quotations embodied in critical articles and reviews.

This book is a work of non-fiction. Unless otherwise noted, the author and the publisher
make no explicit guarantees as to the accuracy of the information contained in this book
and in some cases, names of people and places have been altered to protect their privacy.

WestBow Press books may be ordered through booksellers or by contacting:

WestBow Press
A Division of Thomas Nelson & Zondervan
1663 Liberty Drive
Bloomington, IN 47403
www.westbowpress.com
1 (866) 928-1240

Because of the dynamic nature of the Internet, any web addresses or links contained in
this book may have changed since publication and may no longer be valid. The views
expressed in this work are solely those of the author and do not necessarily reflect the
views of the publisher, and the publisher hereby disclaims any responsibility for them.

Any people depicted in stock imagery provided by Getty Images are models,
and such images are being used for illustrative purposes only.
Certain stock imagery © Getty Images.

The writings of Mother Teresa of Calcutta © by the Mother Teresa
Center, exclusive licensee throughout the world of the Missionaries of
Charity for the works of Mother Teresa. Used with permission.

Scripture quotations are taken from the New King James Version®. Copyright
© 1982 by Thomas Nelson. Used by permission. All rights reserved.

ISBN: 978-1-9736-9276-8 (sc)
ISBN: 978-1-9736-9278-2 (hc)
ISBN: 978-1-9736-9277-5 (e)

Library of Congress Control Number: 2020909621

Print information available on the last page.

WestBow Press rev. date: 6/15/2020

DEDICATION

This book is dedicated to Children of the World

DEDICATION

This book is dedicated to
Children of the World

FADING MEMORIES
HERRING HISTORY

nheriting genes from your ancestors may be scientific —but more important one inherits the challenges of life with love, courage, determination, and hard work for survival.

(1845)"Great Famine of Great Hunger" caused by potato blight which was a fungus disease resulting in dry brown rot of potato tubers. "The German farmers had tried to salvage their food supply with no results causing millions of people to die from starvation. To add to the misery higher taxes were enforced and political censorship led to the revolution in Germany.

Heinrich Herring sat in his rocking chair with loving eyes on his family and smelling the aroma of German wiener schnitzels always cooked perfectly by his devoted wife Maria; but their future weighed heavy on his heart. Earlier Heinrich had listened to his fellow workers at the local tavern concerning emigration to America: escaping the starvation problem, government initiating higher taxes, rising grain prices, overpopulation causing restrictions on marriages, allowing only three religions in the country, and increasing land prices. The property owners were contemplating selling their land to purchase passage to America. Reports from families & friends in America gave positive reports and stated cheap land was available for the newcomers. Since Comanche Chief Santa Anna signed peace treaties in 1849 that allowed German Emigration Company to settle lands north of Llano River, Heinrich had been approached by this company to sign a contract for land in the state of Texas. But his main priority was his family and protecting them by facing the challenges ahead. Recognizing the political views of Sam Houston being past President of Texas, and now governor of Texas also swayed his decision. James Polk served as U.S. President from 1845-1849 and was a fighter for the common people.

His children 12 year old Henry, who was wise above his years; pretty- petite blond 11 yr. old Anna always helping her mom with a smile; and adventurous 6 year old Andrew without a care in the world would face the trip with an exciting positive attitude but accepting leaving his pet pigs would be a heartache. .BUT knowing Andrew, he would accept the adventure with wild ideas of pirates and Indians.

After several sleepless nights, Heinrich discussed the voyage with Maria contemplating a more successful life in America. It was mutually decided and the next morning the family packed only required personal belongings and left their home in Oberkaufungen, Germany in the district of Hesse-Kassel in 1846. The most difficult strain was leaving family especially Maria's sixteen year old daughter by her first marriage who would be staying with family. Maria focused her eyes and heart to her daughter, Martha, with a loving hug hoping this would not be the last reunion. Martha, a mature young lady fought back tears trying to support her Mother

MS. JOYCE SMITH

for the voyage. Sadly, this would be the final episode of their life together.

Heinrich and his family left Oberkaufungen in the district of Kassel with $655.00 in the year 1846. He had experience as a beer brewer and cellar master for wine; but was anxious for new opportunities in Texas. The family left on a wooden sailing ship from Brake, Germany, and upstream on the Weser River. (Wooden sailing ships of that day were small enough to embark upstream.) Andrew was in high heaven wishing for a fishing pole. Henry would not leave his Mother's side knowing she was still depressed leaving her daughter Martha with paternal grandparents. Heinrich embraced Anna who seemed to be confused and worried about the trip. . They arrived at the Bremerhaven Port located downstream from the North Sea.

The Bremerhaven Port was a scene only an admiral and his crew could understand! Germans traveled on ships, trains and roads to the port; but the number of wooden carts with passengers and belongings was a picture of mass emigration.. Andrew made the comment it reminded him of his famous Hog Swine Herd waiting for their dinner. Knowing Andrew was missing the pet pigs, his Mother gave him a hug with an understanding nod.

The vessel was scheduled to leave the following day. The inns were booked and the Herrings met another challenge and survived on the docks with other families. Stories were shared and Andrew loved every conversation soaking in the tales of America.

Early the next morning Andrew scouted the dock and had already met a group of young people that would be sailing to America. He was a good looking young chap of seven years; and was like a magnet making friends never meeting a stranger. Returning to his family with a smile of adventure and his pack on his back; he was ready for the sea. Andrew joked with his brother stating you might have to climb Jacob's ladder...stating it was a substitute made out of rope to board a ship- but Henry only shook his head at his brother and stated maybe they will use you in the Crow's Nest and you can climb Jacob's ladder to heaven! There was not much one could put over Henry!

AHOY-AHOY!

Maria was not prepared for the hardships on the ship and worried constantly about the health of her family. Being sea sick was minor with the smell of spoiled food causing a shortage of food and cholera from contaminated water. The stench of body waste was a problem of its own. Sleeping in close quarters, Maria felt the cold body of Anna and her instincts knew her daughter was possibly suffering from cholera. Maria had heard the cries of a Mother who had lost one of her children from cholera; and her body was trembling with fear as she woke her husband. Heinrich knew to control the diarrhea with warm tea and warm water using warm cotton flannel to keep the body relaxed and warm. They had been on the vessel for 15 days and was hoping they would arrive at the Galveston port within a week. The brothers rationed their water for Anna but Andrew kept at his brother's side wanting security that their little sister would be o.k. . Anna's little body began to have relief whenever the warm winds along the coastline of the voyage to Galveston proved to be the best medication for her recovery. Maria gave strict instruction for her to remain in bed until the ship finished the voyage. Anna like any young girl took advantage of her brothers waiting on her and playing silly games. Henry was patient; but Andrew again could not cope with the crowded quarters but made promises to repeat the stories told on the upper deck.

The family was healing both physically and emotionally. Andrew was on the upper deck whenever the port of Galveston appeared; and overwhelmed with joy his young voice bellowed throughout the ship for the entire vessel to hear the good news. Stumbling over barrels and sprinting to the lower deck, he hugged Anna telling her "everything was going to be o.k."

Leaving the vessel was a reward of its own! Maria was so anxious to bathe and wash the remaining clothes of her family. Her German customs would always be a part of her life and "cleanliness next to Godliness" was at the top of her list! Surprisingly Heinrich spied some long lost friends from Germany, and with gratitude he stated: REPUBLIC OF TEXAS WILL BE OUR NEW HOME with land and a new beginning. The news was still exciting about the annexation of Texas in 1845 and his proud friends boasted of being early pioneers for Texas!

Settling in Brenham, Texas proved to be prosperous for the Herring family. Heinrich had received 640 acres by virtue of colonist contract but traded the land for acres in Washington County. The language barrier was somewhat difficult but the children learned quickly and it pleased them to teach their parents. Home schooling was important before schools were established in Texas. Curious Andrew was always questioning ownership of land in America since the Indians were here before the immigrants. An answer was never available. U.S. President Polk had invoked the concept of Manifest Destiny stating the settlement of the West should be pursued. Andrew questioned the destiny of Indians and the outcome of their future. Being nomads- most of the peaceful Indian tribes never left Texas.

Gold was discovered in California in 1848 with the adventurous leaving Texas for the "Big Strike"; but Heinrich was determined to become a citizen of Texas.

Heinrich worked for five years to receive his citizenship and his dedicated labor of farming proved to be a positive recommendation for becoming an American. He became successful in Texas agriculture owning 640 acres which in many ways was different from the customs in Germany. He learned the English language and was a member of the Lutheran Church.

Appreciative of a new beginning in America, Maria was confused when South Carolina (1860) decided to withdraw from the union that inspired other states to secede including Texas in 1861 due to the slavery issue. News of Abe Lincoln was always positive and was elected U.S. President in 1860 but was shot in 1865. "Honest Abe" wanted freedom for all and even passed a bill to observe last Thursday in November to thank God for all of our blessings and show respect for others. Maria emotionally suffered through the civil war with Texas being part of the confederacy and her son Andrew volunteered his services. Maria was a true Texas Pioneer dying on August 29, 1867 being buried at Ebenezer Lutheran Church in Berlin, Texas.

After his wife died, he suffered through the victims of slavery and the reconstruction of Texas. "Cotton Kingdom" was successful and he prospered with his brother in the late 1880's but continually missing sweet Maria and of course her wiener schnitzels. Their three children were all married and faithfully enjoyed the presence of his grandchildren. Heinrich died in 1892 at the age of 88 and is buried by his wife (Maria) in Berlin, Texas.

The years passed quickly and Andrew (youngest son of Henry and Maria) married Fredericka Miller in 1861 whereas Henry and Anna had already married. Andrew and Fredericka had two children including Mary, the oldest and surviving child of this marriage in 1862. Andrew had volunteered for service in the Civil War because the cotton industry in southern states depended on free labor for agriculture; the northerners wanted to abolish slavery and election of Abe Lincoln who was antislavery put a pressure on southern states; other causes included federal rights versus states; economy whereas the North was becoming more modernized with railroads, canals, newspapers, and transportation; the attack on Ft. Sumter by rebels causing 11 states to secede from the union was the last straw. Andrew felt the need to protect the cotton industry and was stationed only seven miles north of Brenham near his family and was home for the birth of his daughter, Mary. In 1864, Andrew rejoined the 4th Infantry Texas State Troops as a teamster at Camp Cedar Lake, Matagorda County. December, 1864 he received word Fredericka had died from childbirth. Andrew was normally strong during heartaches but at the funeral Andrew was stricken by another tragedy. The newborn had been smothered by coats while the baby was sleeping in the cloak-closet. Andrew's decision was to have the baby buried with his wife; both tragedies caused severe headaches for a period of time after the death of his wife and daughter. (oral history from Aunt Opal (Herring) Bouldin)

Andrew's second marriage was Sophia Kettler on Dec.20, 1865. Andrew & Fredericka had a little girl from his first marriage, (Mary Herring). Andrew and Sophia had 11 children: August, Andrew, Emma, Robert, Louise, Lena, Malinda, Alma, Ida, Bertha, Dora.

The Brazos River Region was noted for the dark, rich soil of the black land prairie proved to be ideal for growing cotton. Like the black gold-oil-that would be discovered later, the soil attracted a rush of immigrants, bringing with them their distinctive cultures. After the Civil War, these settlers transformed this area into one of the most productive cotton-growing regions in the nation.

Andrew gained experience working with his brother, Henry, in the cotton gin but faced another tragedy with his first born son, August (age 10). In 1880 the process of a cotton gin was simple but dangerous.(Story told by Aunt Opal). The cotton bolls were dumped into the hopper and a simple motor turned a cylinder with wire teeth to pull the cotton past a grate. The slots in the grate allow the cotton, but not its seeds to pass through. Second cylinder with brushes pulls the cotton off the toothed cylinder and sends it out of the gin. Samuel, a free slave, admired by August who listened curiously of his stories as a slave and knew he could gain knowledge concerning cotton. . Samuel had always supervised August to be cautious but left for a few minutes to relieve himself. August was anxious to watch the cotton bolls being dumped in the hopper followed by the wire teeth to separate the seeds. But temptation proved to be a serious accident. . Samuel heard the screaming and his instincts knew his small friend was in trouble. August's shirt was caught in the cylinder and the wire teeth demolished his right arm. Samuel cradled him in his arms and with fear in his eyes gave him to Andrew. The parents and Samuel waited for a diagnosis; but amputation was necessary for this young boy and months of healing put a black cloud on the family. Samuel carried the burden and Andrew was never the same after this accident. Andrew eventually sold his farm land and investment in his brother's cotton gin to buy more acres in the new frontier for much less price per acre. It was Andrew's hope moving to West Texas would relieve the pain of his son losing his arm and the death of his first marriage and daughter; unfortunately the pain would always be a part of his life.

On the trip to Runnels and Coleman Counties for his first land purchases in 1886; Andrew was accompanied by his eldest son, August. Indian raids were not as prevalent due to the organization of the Texas Rangers; but robbers and gangs proved to be a major problem. Making the journey from Washington County to Runnels/Coleman Counties would be a challenge. Andrew instructed August to ride the shaggy horse and put the money in his saddle bag. Viewing a young boy on an old horse with one arm would hopefully be of no interest to anyone looking for money. Their route was part of the Chisholm Trail and one night camping with cowboys driving longhorn cattle to market was a history lesson August would never forget. After the Civil War, more than 10 million cattle were herded out of Texas in one of the greatest migrations of animals ever known. The cattle drives laid the foundation for Texas' wildly successful cattle industry and helped elevate the state out of post-Civil War despair and poverty .The "cowpunchers" told stories of their drive to Abilene, Kansas and August learned the vocabulary of "biscuit shooters", "pot rasslers", and "belly cheaters" were nicknames for the trail cook's food. A concoction of raisins and rice became known as "spotted pup", desert was christened "shivering Liz", beans were "prairie whistles", and coffee was "belly wash". The trip was long and viewing the sunset was a welcome sight. August knew he could tend to his horse, stretch his legs, eat a good meal, and a good night's sleep remembering the "tales of the cattle drivers" and the campfire ballad of "The Old Chisholm Trail"-

The remaining journey proved successful without too many hardships. Sore tail, hunger, fatigue, rattlesnakes, coyotes, and trusting strangers were only a few problems they had to endure.

Andrew made his first purchase of 14,000 acres of land in Runnels County, October 1, 1886. Railroad in Runnels/ Coleman County created the town of Talpa, Texas for railroad stop which helped his business. Additional land was purchased later. Andrew Herring was mostly a land man rather than a livestock man as he would buy land, hold it for a while, maybe develop it, and then sell it. According to the Runnels County records, Herring purchased 25,535 acres between October 1, 1886 and his death in 1905. (Herring Facts by :E.Dale Herring, July 23, 2012)

Andrew was born in Oberkaufungen, Hessen, Germany on October 3, 1840 and died May 15, 1905 in Mineral Wells, Texas from cirrhosis of liver hoping the Mineral Spring would cure his sickness. Andrew is buried in the Herring Cemetery in Talpa, Texas beside his second wife, Sophia, who died in 1922. Great Grandfather Andrew "did not mind taking a chance" proving his success in Texas.'

Grandfather August Herring was born on December 31, 1868 and died on August 2, 1933. Even though he had lost his arm, August was successful in life and nothing seemed to stop him from performing well. August was involved in ranching with high interest in registered cattle. Eva Brookshire Herring (wife) was born on January 25, 1880 and died February 23, 1942. Eva was a busy homemaker and was well known for her quilt designs. Eva and August began their early courtship passing notes to each other at Norwood School in Runnels County, Texas. The first child of August and Eva was a son named Price. He was born on March 13, 1900 and died March 30, 1900. The second child was also a son named Hubbard who was born on March 13, 1901 and died on June 3, 1901. A possible stomach infection took both of their lives but diphtheria could have caused their deaths. The inscription on their tiny graves reads "Weep not Papa and Mama for me; I am waiting in heaven for thee".

Uncle Elo: The third child of August and Eva was a son named Elo born in 1904 and died on October 4, 1929. Elo graduated from Talpa High School. Living and working on the ranch, Elo was the arm that August had lost in an accident. He was a "country boy" and loved every minute working on the ranch. Talpa citizens called him the best rancher in Runnels/Coleman counties of Texas. Elo traveled to South America to buy cattle but contracted a disease from "cattle ticks". When he returned his leg started turning black and Dr. Bailey of Coleman, Texas stated it had to be removed but Elo stated, " I would rather die than only have one leg". He knew the hardships his Father had to endure. Elo told his brother (Boss] to take good care of his horse, Hero, if he did not make it. Elo lived three days after the operation and died at the age of 25. . At the funeral his youngest sister (Jo) could not understand what was going on and she got in the casket trying to wake Elo with a favorite song of "Dough Boy". He is buried in the Herring Cemetery beside Price and Hubbard.

Aunt Opal was the fourth child of August and Eva born on October 4, 1907 and died May 26, 1999. Papa Herring would have Priscilla Day make hats for his first daughter because she was so cute. Opal was raised in Talpa and graduated from Talpa High School at the age of 19. She would quilt for hours with her Mother using cotton cords to bind their quilts. She married Charles Bouldin and would sew for the public to supplement the household income. She received fifty cents for a dress and sold "silk stockings & underwear" and was known as the "peddler of silk." Since she could not have children, her family consisted of her dogs, Ted, Bugle Ann, Bob, Chipper and numerous nephews and nieces. Aunt Opal loved new cars and paid $ 600.00 for a 1936 dodge. Her husband died after a long illness in 1964 and she worked in a hospital for 10 years before her death. .This lady never seemed to meet a stranger and her verbal communication with others was always above mediocrity. Aunt Opal lifted the spirits of everyone she came in contact with even if they did not want to listen.

Hubert: (Uncle Boss) the fifth child of August & Eva Herring was born on July 14, 1909 and died on February 2, 1966. It has been noted that Uncle Boss always had a cigar in his mouth and a little Shetland pony tied to his wrist. Boss was an excellent rancher raising cattle and horses. His pastures were neatly cultivated and grub digging any mesquite that sprung on his land. The mystery of Uncle Boss' death is still a cold case. His wife had left him and was already involved with another man. Boss was found in his east tank with rocks tied to him. Uncle Boss never learned how to swim---so why would he put rocks on his neck? The sheriff ruled it as "suicide drowning". There was a disagreement of the land; but sweet Helen (only child of Boss & Grace) with the help of the family the battle was won and she received her inheritance.

Stella: (Aunt Sister) the sixth child of August and Eva born on January 3, 1912 and died June 23, 2011. When Aunt Sister was a young lady she and her friend were driving through Valera, Texas, and a young boy was shooting at cars on the highway. A small bullet entered her ear and the doctor stated it would be better to leave it lodged in her brain because it was such a difficult operation. This did not stop this determined lady. She became a news reporter for the Coleman, Texas paper. Aunt Opal stated "she could pick cotton cleaner than anyone in Texas; and she could make lye soap better than the Tide Company. She raised parakeets; produced the best garden in Runnels County; and worked at several hospitals. She was a patient at Holiday Nursing Home in Coleman winning blue ribbons for her needlework until her death at the age of 99. Aunt Sister married Boyd McClure on February 9, 1933; but divorced him after her three sons were grown. Harold Wayne McClure was born June 22, 1934; Dayton McClure born on September 18, 1937 and died from a stroke in 1916; Sidney Frank McClure was born on May 19, 1939: but died an early death from cancer in 1972.

Donnie Mae: (Mother) was the seventh child of August and Eva Herring born on Armistice Day, November 11, 1917. Donnie Mae was an excellent tennis player and would have been a professional but at the age of 17 she married Tom Bomar whom she kept "in line" for 55 years. In 1942, WWII Daddy was drafted to the Marines and left Mother with four children. She could stretch a dollar at the grocery store to feed her off springs. Being a good cook, she could make oatmeal in various ways and it always taste better than the last batch; and fried chicken soaked in buttermilk could compete with Colonel Sanders any day! "Kid Feeders" was her awarding recipe for desserts by making a chocolate icing and pouring it between two saltine crackers. During World War II her social life consisted of playing canasta with friends and smoking "Lucky Stripes Cigarettes". Rations were given to families during World War II and Talpa people were always generous giving her gas and sugar rations since the oldest son, Rex was diagnosed with polio.

Daddy served his country during World War II. Due to the Selective Training and Service Act of 1940 requiring men who had reached their 21st birthday but had not reached their 36th birthday must register with the local draft. Men could take a choice between "A" or "M" and Daddy selected MARINES. United States became involved in World War II after Japanese attached Pearl Harbor in Hawaii. The attack occurred after United States refused to continue trading iron and gasoline to Japan. General Eisenhower (later President of U.S) had a successful attack on Normandy Coast and liberated Paris. The allied powers consisted of: United States, United Kingdom, France, Soviet Union, Australia, Canada, Belgium and China. The axis alliance consisted of: Germany, Italy, Japan, Hungary, Romania, and Bulgaria. The destruction of Berlin, Germany under the leadership of Hitler ended the war and Japan surrendered. WW11: Daddy was allowed to come home early due to sickness of son and four children. He was a hard worker and supported his family with two or three jobs at one time. He worked for the highway department, ranch work raising sheep and cattle; and was known as the "fastest sheep shearer" in Texas.

Carrie: (Aunt Cacky was the eighth daughter of August and Eva Herring). She could outwork any man and did it to perfection! She married Bunn Jeffreys and two children were born from this marriage. Jo Carolyn (Tootie) and Ronnie. Tootie was not afraid of anyone and needless to say had a few disagreements at school; but we laughed at her courage. Ronnie was usually silent but always had a smile for everyone.

Joine: (Aunt Jo was the ninth child of August and Eva Herring).She married Arnold Allcorn and two fine boys were born of this marriage. The family admired Aunt Jo for completing her nursing degree at a later age after the boys were raised. Uncle Arnold was easy-going and always had "bit of history" in his conversations. Charles, after retiring from Feed Business became a rancher with inheritance from Herring Land. Benny, a successful funeral home director and presides as a minister for funerals.

Living in the big city of Talpa, Texas was at one time at least 500 people and everybody knew everyone! The only crime I can remember was my Grandfather selling liquor illegally and a prisoner escaping from Coleman Jail. We felt safe in our community and if anyone did anything wrong- the entire community knew about it.

Since Mother had inherited land from the Herring Estate, the family moved to the country. Mother raised chickens, turkeys, helped the boys with their pigs, milked the cow each morning, and her garden was compared to the GREEN GIANT and always producing, She kept the family clothed by sewing at night using feed sacks. Daddy and the boys built a two bedroom small house with a wooden stove; using kerosene lamps to read and complete homework. Whenever we returned from school, we knew she would have the doughnuts ready. A country woman with a "heart of gold". Daddy never took advantage of mother. Examples: The family was trying to pen the cattle and since Mother had on a red blouse-he said that was the trouble-so she took it off . The cattle drivers were shock but had a good laugh. Daddy never opened his mouth the rest of the day! Mother was a super cook and took pride in her menus. Sunday dinner with fried chicken and mashed potatoes with homegrown corn was a feast anyone would enjoy. Mother was so busy making the gravy she forgot the biscuits; they burned and when put on the table Daddy questioned the color. Mother picked up each burned biscuit and threw everyone at him and said, "Pick your favorite color". Of course- the siblings were dodging the biscuit ball game. Our parents taught us to be responsible and it was understood if the "work schedule" was not completed there would not be "swimming," "fishing", "coon hunting" "horseback riding" or "having friends over"! The long marriage produced six children: Thomas Rex (May-31, 1935); Jimmie Dale (Oct. 14, 1936); Eva Joyce (Feb.7, 1939) Author of this non-fiction novel; Billie Pat (March 21, 1940); Gary Don (Jan. 15, 1951); and Vickie Darlene, Oct. 28, 1957.

Living in the country with four brothers was revelry. Hunting varmints of any kind with a spotlight at night usually produced good skins to sell-especially the fox. Skunks were a different story! The boys and I were looking for minnows in a nearby creek and an ole skunk came roaming from a mesquite tree; the boys dared me to catch it and trying to be just like her brothers-I gave it a try. Of course everyone was sprayed and whenever we returned home Mother poured tomato juice on us and we sat in the mud at our swimming hole. Needless to say- we went to bed hungry. Fishing and swimming in the tank was at the top of our amusement list. Rex and Jimmie loved to rope goats and Pat and I were responsible for opening the gate and rounding them up for the many roping events. Five of us attended a very small school in Talpa,Texas; and the cafeteria cook was our Grandmother who gave us special attention.

Rex was number #1 baseball catcher and also #1 receiving the most demerits and spankings from Superintendent

Mitchell. Rex was mischievous always thinking of pranks from turning over outdoor toilets to borrowing watermelons. He did attend college at Sul Ross State University; but outdoor work was his major. He worked in the oilfields and eventually moved to Midland, Texas owning his business. He had two marriages father of three boys from first marriage (Jackie, Kenny, and Shane) and one boy (Randy) from second marriage. After Rex's death, his wife, Patsy, moved to Ballinger, Tex. and their son continues to raise cattle on the Bomar Ranch south of Talpa.

Jimmie, exceled in baseball as first basement and played 6 Man football and was offered a scholarship from Tarleton State College in Texas for his athletic abilities. Eventually he transferred to Sam Houston being a part of the cowboy clubs and probably drinking his share of beer. North Korea and South Korea had their differences an 1956 and Jim was drafted in the Korean War and sent to Germany to help the U.S. forces. Main cause of this war was communism and President Truman stated the U.S. will help any country that is threatened by this act. In 1950, North Korea invaded South Korea at a spot called 38th parallel. Russia controlled North Korea and United States controlled South Korea. General Douglas Mac Arthur leads an invasion and United Nation troops protected South Korea. South Korea and North Korea signs an agreement to stop fighting and the two are separated by neutral zone called Demilitarized Zone. Stationed in Germany-Jim met his "perfect" Fraulein (Barbara). Barbara was always doing for others, a champion playing "scrabble, but her favorite phrase for cocktail hour was "It's five o'clock somewhere". The couple lived in California working in the feed yards and moved back to Texas for Jim to accept the position as President of Walco Veterinary Corp. Oldest boy, Ricky, was adopted by Jimmie; and Pam & Tommy were their biological children. Barbara died of bone cancer and her absence brought sadness Jimmie died of a heart attack using his last days to be a successful investor. As far as I know, the only serious argument between the two was when Barbara cut down a tree near her swimming pool; otherwise, a very healthy marriage.

Pat, 13 months younger than myself, was always ready to lift a helping hand for his sister. We always considered him as the sweet family member and was never in trouble. He did well in sports, 4H projects and his creative skills were unbelievable which helped him become a success. Pat eloped in Mexico with his high school sweetheart, Linda, as soon as he graduated from high school. Since Linda had not finished school, she bravely returned and graduated. The couple lived at the Big Ranch for a while and moved to Ballinger to greet their first son, Bill. They moved to Denton to greet their second son, Tony. Pat worked for many years as a roofer until Mr. Max (owner) died and he bought the business. They did well and was able to retire on a lake in North Texas with time to hunt, fish, golf and Linda continues her volunteer work for St. Jude's hospital.

Gary was the youngest son and could outdo his siblings on occasions; but learning the livestock work from Daddy was at the top of his list. He continues taking care of the Bomar Ranch and enjoys hunting deer and elk. He said "learning from Tom Bomar" was a challenge and an enjoyment. Being involved with 4H and raising show animals was still his priority; but receiving the EAGLE BOY SCOUT honor proved his upbringing. His credentials with a major from A & M landed him a job as a District County Agent in the agriculture field. Gary was the father of two girls from his first marriage (Donna Jo & Kelli). He has become a caregiver to his second wife, Marcy, who is suffering from Parkinson. The family admires him for enduring the accomplishments of excellent skills in the Agriculture field, managing the ranch, household duties, and taking care of Marcy with patience- he will be blessed.

Vickie was a late bloomer being the youngest of the group by twenty three years difference from oldest brother, Rex. We spoiled her rotten and she had Daddy wrapped around her little finger. Mother was patient, kind, and had more time with her younger children. Moving to Ballinger as a baby, Vic had more opportunities of social life: Brownie troop with Mother as the leader, Cheerleader, sport activities, and enjoying her teen-age years with many friends. Vickie and her husband were high school sweethearts and married after high school graduation and with determination they both graduated from college. Two girls, Ashley and Janda were a blessing for this couple. Vic traveled with her coaching husband in various schools in Texas and was labeled as a "good coaching wife" and received an honor for her participation in the sports world.

(Joyce-last but not least) was considered the third child- but always thought she was first being the only girl for 18 years. Her independence proved to be a greater challenge in her life; and was labeled unorthodox who does what it takes to get things done with a stubborn streak –of course. Country living teaches responsibility and creativity but we were punished when it was necessary. We had chores but we also had freedom. Shopping in grocery store one evening I noticed Daddy picking up grapes and eating them off the shelf; being only 10 years old, a decision was made to obtain a sack and fill it to the brim. Eating the grapes with the knowledge of store owner; it was asked if I had paid for the grapes. Turning toward Daddy, I stated: "did you?" Well, that was the wrong question. Arriving home, a large sack of grapes were given to me to eat every one and was sick for a week with diarrhea. To this date, stealing is remembered with each bite of grapes. Even backing the car and bending the fender brought a chore of "Huckleberry Finn" and it took almost a week of hard labor to paint the home fence. The punishment of not being able to go swimming until the job was done made it even worse.

Our family of six had a traveling vacation to Wyoming in an old Chevy packed to the gill. I remember the beauty of Old Faithful Geyser in Yellowstone Park. Being siblings, we had a few disagreements traveling; Mother tried to teach us the Golden Rule, but I can still hear her saying: "As God is my witness if you do not straighten up- we are going to leave you on the highway and please recall there are bears in Wyoming". (At the time all I could think of was mean bears instead of mean brothers.)

Learning to swim was easy. Daddy threw me in the creek and said "swim". I did and taught this sport teaching children at Church Camps and giving private lessons to children. Building tree houses was fun as an individual until tarantula spiders invaded my little home; but thank goodness for little brother who saved the day! The "Bomar Gang" had a horse called Shorty and bless his heart how he put up with us switching riders is a mystery. Riding the bike was a hobby and finally after much begging; Mother finally gave permission to pedal that bike six miles to see my Talpa friends. Coming home after a full day of fun, it was a welcome sight to see Mother at the edge of town waiting on patiently for a tired bike rider. Sadly, as we know, it would be too dangerous for a 12 year old to be on the country roads for hours. How times have changed!

The Talpa School was small and everyone knew everyone. With seven classmates and three of them were cousins, we always made sure we defended our relatives. Basketball was my favorite sport and did win several awards in the district. Cheerleader, football queen, festival queen, plays, favorite of the class were a few honors; but the school was small so there were not many opponents. Mr. Glynn Mitchell was also our parents' superintendent and knew the Bomar family well. He was strict but honest and always gave a report to our parents. One morning my friends and I had a pow-wow and decided it would be fun if we played "HOOKEY" the next day. Sitting on the railroad track and laughing how we fooled everyone until Mr. Mitchell appeared....we received "swats" and a call to parents received more swats that evening. (CPS would have fainted!) School was fun because we were all friends; therefore few disagreements happened on our campus. Dancing in private homes, slumber parties, pulling silly pranks and moving outdoor toilet made an interesting week-end. Living in the country in the 50's learning the facts of life from animals and nature and living on God's land taught us respect and independence. An explanatory remark: "We had fears in our life, but it wasn't because of drive-by shootings, drugs, gangs, sexual assaults, or protestors—our PARENTS and GRANDPARENTS were a bigger threat. We survived because of their love was greater than a threat." Our parent s were protective of us and had definite rules for being accountable for our actions. (Family stories from Donnie Mae Herring Bomar:)

Texas Tech College (1957) opened a new world!. Pledged a sorority but was not accustomed to dealing with the silly chores; and considered it a clique more than honest friendships. Marcia, first roommate, was dedicated to her studies and synchronize swimming. More action was needed and meeting Laine has been compared to Lucy & Ethel because we loved to have fun. "Pantie Raid" was popular in the fifties and we collected the second floor dorm panties and headed for the basement to throw at the football players. BUT we were caught red-handed and put on probation for six weeks. We loved to date with the Sigma Nu Fraternity and one particular man made it even more fun. I was selected Sigma Nu Queen in 1958 with many parties to end the semester and also ended my semester at Texas Tech with low grades. So the two friends enrolled at Sam Houston State College and was determined to raise their grade point. Sam Houston was known for good looking football players and we made sure they knew us. Dollar, football player, was my best friend and we had some good times together; but Charlie, the shy one, was a challenge and a respected "soul mate" being thoughtful but not committed to a relationship. One evening skiing on Lake

Livingston I was acting smart and fell dislocating my hip. Charlie was the first to dive in and pull me to shore. After the healing process with crutches, he always had a helping hand to attend my classes. They don't make anyone like "Charlie".

College life in 50's and 60's was different from high school and we were always aware of young men making advances. We let them know our rules and always set it straight we were not to be used; and if they did not agree-"Good-by Joe Blow". Meeting true friends was the backbone of college life. Now as Senior Citizens we have cruised the Caribbean, rented a cabin in Ruidoso, flew to Oregon touring the coastline lighthouses, regular summer visits to a beach home in Galveston, celebrated our 50th anniversary in Phoenix, and of course visits to my Lil Ranch to listen and solve our problems of becoming older and hopefully wiser; and we always Thank GOD for the beauty of friendship.

Dr. King, a sociology professor, assigned the students prisoners from Huntsville State Prison and a women's prison to interview as part of the curriculum. Candy Barr was my prize at the Huntsville State Prison in Texas for women. Her sentence entailed drugs and prostitution using her beauty and brain to increase her savings account. For six weeks I listened and learned while the talented artist painted outstanding pictures of prison life and sad pictures of her background in her earlier life. Admiration was given to her for her honesty and friendliness. Dr. King posted an "A" for the interesting interviews with Candy Barr. Candy died in Dallas, Texas after she was released but her name is still in the history logs.

After graduating from Sam Houston State College, I accepted a position at San Antonio County as a probation officer for juvenile delinquents. The time spent in San Antonio proved to be an awakening to the problems young people faced every day. Young boys and girls involved in drugs, truancy, stealing, prostitution and the list goes on but I can honestly say my parents gave me loving experience to deal with "troubled young people". I loved the job but decided to marry Bill Smith in 1961.

We were blessed with two children, George Wm.(09-21-1962) and Missy (07-10-1966). My husband was employed with the telephone company and taking inventory was his job. Sherman, Texas was the beginning of our lives being married in the First Methodist Church in 1961. We never unpacked completely because in two years we moved from Sherman-to Dalhart- to Perryton-to Lubbock- to Memphis to Seymour, to Clarendon Texas. My running buddy, Laine, came for a visit and we heard Paul Newman was shooting a movie called "Hud". So the two set our alarms for 6:00 A.M. and drove 30 miles down the road to watch the filming at Claude, Texas. They were asking for "extras" and of course we applied to be in the film. Being 7 months pregnant disqualified me. Laine, true friend, passed the invitation. We did visit with "ole Blue Eyes" which proved exhilarated.

George William was born in Lubbock; PaPaw & Nanny were his first visitors and Mother and Vickie came to help. Moving to Dalhart with rent houses hard to find- but we found a small house near a bar with colored lights beaming at night. Our young son loved every "blinking light" and proved to be a sleeping device. November 22, 1963, rocking George Wm. and watching the soap opera "As The World Turns" when breaking news stated John Kennedy our 35th president was assassinated by Harvey Lee Oswald in Dallas while riding in a presidential parade. Oswald was charged with murder and was being transferred to county jail when Jack Rudy gunned him down.

We decided to settle in San Angelo but working for the insurance company did not pay the bills; and this was the beginning of Bill's drinking knowing the family was important so he rejoined the army after serving in the fifties. I accepted a job with the Girl Scouts of America being district advisor for four counties and six schools in San Angelo, Texas. The leaders in Eldorado, Menard, Junction, and Mason were "top of the crop" and being pregnant they treated me like a queen.. The highlight of working with the Girl Scout Program was the outdoor life of camping. Day Camps were scheduled for the Brownies to teach basic techniques; and Mo Ranch Girl Scout Camp offered more advanced skills for two weeks. Girl Scout cookies were $.50 a box in 1966! Times have changed......

In 1966 Missy came into our lives with a few problems. Missy was early and considerate Dr. Moon (GYN) slept in the room with me hoping child birth would be natural but delivered Missy with a broken arm. Since her father was already stationed at Ft. Wolters, he came the next day to see this little curly-hair beautiful girl with a cast that healed quickly. While living in San Angelo, Papaw made it a point to spoil George William, Smiths gave full attention to their first grandchild and Bomars gave continuous attention to Missy. Since George William was older, Papaw would take him to work and shop at the grocery store and also would go to Nanny's Dress shop to visit Ms. Hassell, a beloved older woman that loved him as much as he loved her. Missy loved to go to her maternal grandparents because they spoiled her. They were both loved by both grandparents. (Info from personal experience of Author)

Military Family::

A truly blessing to be part of the military when my husband joined the army and trained for a warrant officer flying helicopters. Our first leg of training was at Ft. Wolters, Mineral Wells, Texas. Missy was hospitalized with pneumonia and we were fortunate to hire a private black loving nurse (whom she loved dearly) to take care of her because she kept pulling out her IV. She was back to normal in a couple of weeks but always asking for her nurse. Military people are labeled as friends for a lifetime and this was true whenever I met my friend, Ginny. We traveled several years together and the friendship continued for almost 40 years until cancer took her life. North Carolina was the second leg of our journey and these southern people knew how to make one feel at home. George William would take a tablet and go around the neighborhood introducing himself and writing down their names. Missy, still a baby played with her pet rabbit; and being her playmate we took Fluffy(rabbit) to Ft. Wolters, Texas completing our third leg for training as an Warrant Officer. U.S. Army was involved with Vietnam at this time and many soldiers gave their life to protect us. Vietnam War was officially fought between North Vietnam and South Vietnam. North Vietnam was supported by Soviet Union, China, and other communism countries; South Vietnam was supported by the United States, South Korea, Philippines, Australia, Thailand, and other anti-communist countries. It was considered a "cold war" by many historians because it lasted some 19 years with direct U.S. involvement ending in 1973 following the Paris Peace Accords. It was not unusual for the wives to observe a chaplain knocking on doors to give the sad news; and the military families were the supporters. Bill was sent to Viet Nam, and the three of us moved to an apartment in San Angelo—which delighted PaPaw. Both of them were in a day nursery but George William dreaded going during week and hung on me until I cried too; and begged Papaw to keep him. One night Missy had an accident falling on the bed rail bringing a book for me to read. The blood was coming and I jumped out of bed and told George Wm. to go after Mr. Eldridge (kind neighbor) and we zoomed to hospital noticing I forgot to dress still in my gown. Hospital staff gave me a jacket and laughed. Goodfellow Hospital performed techniques to heal the scar on her face. To supplement the income, I worked as a social worker at the McKnight hospital in Carlsbad, Tex. which was a tuberculosis unit. Being assigned to the children's ward, sometimes it was more than I could handle. Precious children with lung disease but always happy waiting for the story of the day! Releasing children after investigating the home situation for the dismissal was part of my work; but when one of the children died during my investigation it was difficult for the parents- and heart-breaking for me.

MILITARY ADVENTURES

ilitary Adventures: During Vietnam War, the Military soldiers were given the opportunity to travel to Hawaii to meet their families. So for the first time disposal diapers were bought for Missy and George William helped with diaper bag and stroller. While flying, Missy was continuous crying-Wm. tried to entertain her; passengers were sympathetic but a political person from First Class sent word to quite the baby! Well, that did not set right with the passengers and one man let him know about military families. Good people care about children! An apology was given in person to economy class. Arriving in Hawaii Missy was taken directly to doctor and the diagnosis was an ear infection and high attitude flying made it more painful. With proper medicine we had a good time on the beach and even bought matching Hawaiian shirts to remember our time together. The children were too young to remember the military history of Pearl Harbor but it was an overwhelming experience with the tour.

Pearl Harbor is a U.S. Naval Base near Honolulu, Hawaii that was the scene of a devastating surprise attack by Japanese forces on December 7, 1941. On a Sunday morning, hundreds of Japanese fighter planes descended on the base, where they managed to destroy or damage nearly 20 American naval vessels, including 8 battleships, and over 300 airplanes. More than 2400 Americans died in the attack, including civilians and another 1000 people wounded. Japanese planes filled the sky on Pearl Harbor. A 1,800 pound bomb smashed through the deck of USS Arizona. The ship exploded and sank more than 1000 men trapped inside. (U.S. History)

Day after the assault President Franklin D. Roosevelt asked Congress to declare war on Japan. Japan believed the only way to solve their economic problems and demographic problems were to expand into China and take over the import markets. Japan declared war on China in 1937. American officials responded to this aggression with a battery of economic sanctions and trade embargoes. They reasoned without access to money and goods, and especially essential supplies like oil. Japan would have to rein in its expansion. Instead, Japan was more determined to stand their ground. During months of negotiations between Tokyo and Washington D.C.-neither side would budge. War was all but inevitable. Ref:

Back to our story, our 4th leg was returning to Ft. Wolters to complete training and graduate as Warrant Officers. Since the schools were overcrowded, I was needed to teach 4th grade inheriting students that teachers preferred for them to leave. A mixture of personalities but this class proved to be respectful and successful. George Wm. had dental problems and very contentious for his appointments. I had to bribe him in every way! Missy tried to help saying you will be "pretty" but Wm. did not like her remarks. He had a retainer but would take it out and one school day someway it was put in a trash can. We dumped trash from numerous rooms until finally we found it; needless to say he learned to keep it in his mouth. Some babysitters are just plain lazy and sadly we experienced one keeping Missy. Ginny, my friend, kept her to the end of school year. Bill was sent to Vietnam again and the kids and I moved to Ballinger to live near my parents. George William was in second grade and joining the Cub Scouts was a blessing for him. He could not adjust to his father being gone and his Papaw would see to it he received attention making several trips from San Angelo to Ballinger. Missy was an independent toddler but was spoiled by her maternal grandparents. Mother, the perfect seamstress, made her the cutest dresses including her ballerina dress and other costumes and continuously kept her closet voluminous through her elementary years. Bonding with grandparents was a plus for Wm. and Missy!

5th Leg: Ft. Rucker, Alabama. Another friendly southern state but weather was not the best! Seems kids and I plus one German shepherd spent many nights under the bed when tornadoes were bouncing around in Alabama. Bill usually had field duty but we survived! George William was in 3rd grade and involved in sports. Missy, kindergarten, would ride her bike to school even though I was hiding around every corner making sure she made it. Living on a military base was safe; but this cute blond hair little girl would attract anyone. The best surprise was a visit from Grandma Bomar riding a bus from Texas to Alabama with Vickie. It took courage for this senior citizen to make this long trip with her young granddaughter to visit her older granddaughter and great-grandchildren.

6th Leg: Orders for S.H.A.P.E Belgium in Europe

Preparing for the trip to Belgium, as a Mother, I had worry pains not knowing what lay ahead in the next four years. I kept telling the children the advantages of traveling to Europe and learning about new cultures.

General Andrew J. Goodpaster, Supreme Allied Commander Europe had brought to SHAPE the accumulated experience of more than thirty-five years of brilliant and varied service with the United States Army. Bill was fortunate to have been his pilot while in Belgium.

George Wm. accepted the fate since he could be closer to his Dad. Missy was Missy! Landing in Brussels, Belgium would be the beginning of our adventures. The drive to S.H.A.P.E. with no legal speed limits was fast and fury and praying every kilometer for safety. Checking into a hotel while waiting on housing was an adventure meeting different nationalities and making new friends.

Living in close quarters with other families became our "clique" throughout the next four years. We learned to depend upon each other, play bridge, attend parties together, and the friendship overlapped for life. While living in the hotel, I woke in the early A.M. with thriving headache and flu symptoms. Was rushed to hospital and after a spinal tap, the diagnosis was meningitis. The memory of hospital stay were worrying about the children, being packed in ice, headaches, high fever, and strong medications. This sickness proved to be a future cause for an unexpected miscarriage.

Living in Mons, Belgium with the Belgians was more than a history lesson; our landlord Albert, became a lasting friend to the Smith Family. We lived in his three-storied home and his laundry business was located on the block. Albert would visit every day about 4:00 P.M. and we would drink peach brandy which we called my heart medicine; and listen to his stories of being a prisoner in a German camp during World War ll. Belgium involvement in World War II began when German forces invaded Belgium. After 18 days of fighting, Belgium surrendered on 28 May, 1940 and was placed under German occupation. Virtually all the soldiers of the Belgian army who were not killed in action were captured at some point during May, 1940. Belgian prisoners were forced to work in quarries or in agriculture. Conditions were variable, but around 2000 died in captivity, mostly from disease and lack of medical attention. Of the prisoners released in 1945, one quarter were suffering from debilitating diseases, particularly tuberculosis. The most well- known German prisoner of war camps were known as either Stalags (both officers and enlisted soldiers) or

Oflags (officers only). Before being sent to a camp, a captured prisoner of war had to pass through a (Dulag) which were transit camps where details of the prisoners were processed. Under the terms of the Geneva Convention prisoners only had to give details of their name, rank, and serial number. Prisoners would then be transported by train to a prisoner of war camp. At intervals the train would stop and all prisoners would get out of train to either relieve themselves or empty their bowels by the side of the track. Individual camps were enclosed with barbed wire and contained guard towers which was manned by German soldiers ready to shoot if anyone tried to escape. Prisoners were housed in one-story barracks containing bunk beds and a charcoal stove in the middle of the room. Prisoners were usually given two meals a day-thin soup and black bread. All prisoners looked forward to the deliveries of Red Cross food parcels which contained butter, biscuits, chocolate and condensed milk as well as dried fruit and vegetables. However, for most, the overriding features of life in a prisoner camp were boredom, hunger, and dreams of a better life .(Stories from Albert) Albert stated it took him over a year to adjust after prisoner life; but gained weight and opened a successful laundry healing his memories.

Albert knew "antique furniture" was our weakness and he always knew the best auctions; his rule was to keep our "mouth shut" and he would do the bidding and was always successful with good bargains. Albert was fun! One night he and I drove to French border to buy wine on the black market. I was the "lookout person" and I guess looking for police was my job. I really did not know! At the time, we were not thinking about the law- just two friends having fun. We loaded his van and had good wine for an extended time. An invitation to his country home was enjoyable with the guys shooting clay pigeons. His sweet wife who only spoke Flemish and I talked by playing charades and laughed after the words were solved. The food was very different and the appearance was not appealing to Missy & George Wm. but at least they tried to eat the special dishes of uncooked ground meat made with a special sauce. Living in the village of Mons, Belgium put a limit entertaining the children. A room in our Belgium home was cleared of all furniture and very large measurement of ply wood for a miniature railroad track with all types of railcars, depot, railroad characters, lights, small hills, rivers & lakes, passengers, grass, etc. with electric devices to play. Kids loved it and motor skills were improved; but the competition was a factor. An annual interesting festival was the celebration of "Throwing Oranges" bringing good luck from the Giles and was an insult if one threw them back. The kids could not believe the multitude of oranges being thrown at homes and on the streets. The Giles were clad in elaborate costumes and wax masks with sticks to ward off bad spirits. Living in a three-storied home gave us a ring-size seat and protection. The kids did enjoy going to the Bakery and selecting Belgium sweets. Leaving Albert's home in Belgium was rewarding because of the culture. Going away gift of an antique needle point tapestry was given to me by Albert which is a reminder hanging in my home toasting a sincere friend. Good memories of our friend, Albert.

Moving to military housing at S.H.A.P.E: Our home was surrounded by international families. The friendly British lived across the street and their speech was unbelievable especially the phrase "don't get cheeky". Parties with the different nationalities were cultural experiences.

Belgium Adventures: Bruges (Venice of the North) and Brussels Centre with a statue of the Nanneken- P. which is a bronze sculpture depicting a little boy urinating into a fountain basin. "Old wives tale states the little boy was lost and the Father stated he would build a statue of what he was doing at the time he was found!"

George William was on a baseball team and did exceptional well pitching. He did play football and earned a letter jacket in Junior High. Missy was on a swim team & baseball team. Therefore it was necessary to move to the military base because of distance and time. Missy would be at the indoor pool around 6AM and practice until school or would swim after school. She did prove to be the youngest and most improved swimmer on the team with a trophy that is placed at S.H.A.P.E with her recognition. Traveling to various countries competing but most interesting swim meet was in Berlin traveling on a train from the military base. I was only worried about the train not stopping at "Checkpoint Charlie" before we entered the danger zone of Berlin Wall. (The wall was a guarded concrete barrier and ideologically divided Berlin from 1961 to 1969. Constructed by the German Democratic Republic (East Germany). The wall cut off West Berlin from virtually all of East Germany; wall was called "Iron Curtain" or "Wall of Shame" during the "Cold War". (*Berlin Wall) Swim team was allowed to visit the wall; but through the sadness the only good deed was secretly taking a piece of a rock from the wall and storing in my memory chest. Every small deed helps freedom! (Demolition of wall began in 1990 and finished in 1992)

On the road: We had a van with a picture of a duck on the door; so we called it "Duckie Car". First trip with the kids was to Garmisch, Germany to snow ski staying at the Edelweiss Lodge and Resort for military families. George Wm., Missy, and Bill had a "blast", and this was the beginning of kids loving snow skiing. I broke my toe and stayed at the bar drinking wine. We headed north to Austria to view the location of the Olympics in Innsbruck of 1964. Point of interest was the Bergisel Ski Jump constructed for the Olympics; but used for other competitions.

On the road again for trips to France & Spain: Paris, France is noted for culture fashion and art history. World's most beautiful avenue in Paris leads from Arc of Triumph (Monument which honors those who fought in the French Revolution and Napoleon War) into Tuileries Gardens. Points of interest of course was the Eiffel Tower: Wrought iron lattice tower on the avenue Champs de Mars with an architectural feet of 986 and 1,063 tip feet with three levels. The tower is named after architect Gustave Eiffel. Notre Dame Roman Catholic Cathedral with walls that are gold plated with amazing architectural designs are amazing but underground chapel was more interesting.

Louvre Museum is the home of the portrait "Mona Lisa". Mona Lisa is a half-length portrait painting by the Italian artist Leonardo da Vinci. It has been described as "best known", "most visited", "most written about", "most parodied work of art in the world" making it the most famous painting in the world. There is a mystery to this famous painting concerning the exact identity of the "sitter".

The kids asked why she was smiling? (no idea)

Vive la France: Expression used at the end of speeches such as "God Bless Her" and God Save the Queen.

Traveling to Spain but camping in southern France was the highlight of our journey. The beauty of the land with trees that seem to say "welcome". A small lake was nearby and kids enjoyed every splash. We cooked on a campfire, slept in a tent, and enjoyed quiet time with French wine . (Hopefully the kids remembered the beauty of Southern France.)

On the road again: We took Sam our dachshund with us; but Sam did not tolerate the French Cheese and passed gas all the way to Spain. Our windows were constantly rolling up or down. At the time it was not funny but became a humorous story.

ADVENTURES CONT

As parents we felt it necessary for our off-springs to understand European History and we did our best to tour Europe.

Spain has more BLUE FLAG BEACHES than any other country in Europe. Blue Mediterranean Sea stretches for more than 1,000 miles along coastal region of Spain connecting to the Atlantic Ocean.

Traveling to Spain was similar to traveling to Old Mexico. Ordering for lunch were usually Mexican Food plates; but being the curious one Joyce had to try the octopus soup and escargots (delicacy of cooked land snails) and ravened every bite. Reaching our destination at a nice resort called Costa Blanca, we were ready to leave "Duckie Car;" even Sam had to run a block or two to decrease the stiffness from traveling and relieve his constipation. Our accommodations included a private swimming pool, kitchenette, fresh linens, small living area, balcony overlooking the Mediterranean Sea, tours to open market including the fresh fish of your choice but also watching the catches being landed. The kitchenette came in handy after we shopped at the fish market and open market for spices and fresh vegetables. The "broiled shark" was mouth-watering especially with help from the staff. The kids could not wait to go play in the ocean the next day; we took Sam with us throwing his tennis ball in the waves and he would always wait patiently for the ball to come to him. Sam had a "growing audience" and one particular man was filming; and asked what nationality we were and when we stated Americans he unloaded the film and threw it in the ocean. We were confused and still the mystery lingers. Since the temperature is very high in the afternoon, Spain's Siesta (nap) businesses and shops close from 2:p.m. to 5: P.M. Ay siesta time, Bill and I tried to teach the kids how to play bridge. "That went over like a lead balloon"!

On the way home we decided to stop in Pamplona to watch the "running of the bulls"-hilarious demonstration watching the men trying to outrun the bulls. Bull fighting with trained matadors were more of a sport.

Luxembourg Cemetery and Memorial was perfervid visitation: Cemetery is entered between tall iron gates weighing over a ton and bearing gilded laurel wreaths- the ancient award for valor. Watch gate has a cluster of thirteen stars commemorating the original composition of the United States of America, Gilded bronze eagles-and our national emblem. Chapel is built of Valore Stone, quarried in Central France. The dedication reads: IN PROUD REMEMBRANCE OF THE ACHIEVEMENTS OF HER SONS AND IN HUMBLE TRIBUTE TO THEIR SACRIFICES THIS MEMORIAL HAS BEEN ERECTED BY THE UNITED STATES OF AMERICA AND ABOVE THE DEDICATION IS THE Great Seal of the United States. Over the Chapel doorway are inscribed the following words: HERE IS INSHRINED

THE MEMORY OF VALOR AND SACRIFICE. Above, stands the 23 foot Angel of Peace with its right hand raised in blessing, surmounted by the dove.

It is fitting that Luxembourg is represented on the Memorial. A country of 999 square miles and some 350,000 inhabitants, was occupied by enemy forces, into which over 12,000 of the little country's young men were conscripted for service on the Russian front during WWII. One-third of this group were eventually reported as killed or missing in action. It is also understandable that the troops of the U.S. Fifth Armored Division received a joyous welcome when they liberated Luxembourg City (Capital) on 10 September 1944. U.S. Third Army under General George Patton managed not only to liberate Luxembourg the second time, but also to relieve our beleaguered forces holding the town of Bastogne in Belgium. American casualties resulting from the Third Army engagement were brought to this cemetery. In 1945, 8,411 graves and 1949, 5,076 burials because the next of kin exhorted the remains of the dead returned to the U.S. As the year drew to a close, General Patton ("Old Blood and Guts") was injured in an automobile accident in Mainz, Germany. Complications set in and proved fatal; General Patton was interred in this cemetery among his former soldiers on 21 December 1944. One hundred and seventeen graves are marked with the Star of David, indicating that the deceased were of Jewish faith. All other faiths are marked with the Roman Cross. There are also, 101 graves of unknown soldiers or airmen. The headstones marking these graves bear the inscription: HERE LIES IN HONORED GLORY A COMRADE IN ARMS KNOWN BUT TO GOD.

Twenty-two pairs of brothers buried here. Should be noted, General Patton's wife, Beatrice Ayer Patton was cremated and ashes strewn over his grave thus supporting each other after death. A tear in our eyes and a salute to the brave military was an honor to visit this historic cemetery. (Books sold at the cemetery concerning the history)

GERMANY

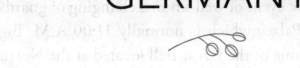

Roaming the Heidelberg Castle was almost as interesting as the recent <u>Harry Potter Books;</u> and listening for ghosts was a mystery of its own. Castle is a ruin in Germany and landmark of Heidelberg are among the most Renaissance structure north of the Alps. Stuttgart, capital and largest city in Germany with Octoberfest Christmas Bazaar selling items of all shapes and forms. Black Forest is a large forested mountain range in SW Germany bounded by the Rhine Valley to west and south. Bremerhaven, city at seaport of Bremen located on the River Weser with a long history of a trade port shipping good German Wine to United States.

ENGLAND: Arriving at Rotterdam to catch the exciting trip to England on a ferry with hyperactive kids who were engrossed watching the ferry paddling through the Strait of Dover and tasting the various food selections at the buffet. Spying the White Cliffs of Dover is intricately linked with white cliffs given to region of English coastline facing the Strait of Dover and France. Cliff reaches a height of 350 feet and owes it appearance to its composition of chalk accented with streaks of black flint. London is the capital and populous city of England and the United Kingdom and standing on River Thames founded by the Romans. (Geography)

Time to Talley-Ho Young Chaps and visit landmarks of

England:(Scheduled tours) (1) Watching Big Ben Clock to schedule a historic event of well-known changing of guards at Buckingham Palace which is normally 11:00 A.M. Big Ben is the nickname of the Great Bell located at the North End of Place of Westminster. Official name was Clock Tower but renamed Elizabeth Tower in 2012 to mark the Diamond Jubilee of Elizabeth II. Queen's Guard and Queen's Life Guard are names given to contingents of infantry and cavalry soldiers charged with guarding the official royal residence in United Kingdom. (2) Hop On and Hop Off Double Decker Buses to continue tour and of course the Texans had to ride at top and laughed at driver "driving on the wrong side of road". (3) First hop off: Scotland Yard being the headquarters of the London Metropolitan Police. The force was created in 1829 and one of the most famous serial killers was "Jack the Ripper" who is most famous for stalking poor women and prostitutes and killing them. There are many theories about the identity of Jack Ripper; the Ripper's identity remains unknown to this date. (4) Tower of London: From medieval TORTURE to grim EXECUTIONS and infamous royal prisoners, the Tower of London has found itself at the center of the city's dark HISTORY. (5) England's Wax Museum is globally acclaimed by Madam Tussauds. Its history is fascinating and its exhibitions HAUNTING in their accurate likeness. Henry VIII and his six wives are examples of wax masterpieces at the museum and murdered two of his wives. Henry VIII was obese and a leg injury kept him from exercising and became ulcerated. It has been stated "he died from drinking too much chocolate milk". (Could happen) (5) Westminster Abbey can be traced back to the

12th century where it was used as a Benedictine Monastery (religious order). The confessor's shrine, the tombs of Kings and Queens and countless memorials and setting for each coronation since 1066. MOMA is a technique that involves pencil, chalk, charcoal, or crayon rubbing onto a sheet of paper that has been placed on top of a textured object or tombstone. Process causes the raised portions of the picture below to be transferred to paper. George William loved to sketch and this was up his "alley" seeing his finishing touches of famous kings and queens. Missy was not impressed with the dead royalty. (6) Tea for Four: "Fancy a Cuppa" meaning would you like a cup of tea? O'Neill's Irish Pub in London with live music and the British are known to be "cheerful" people and the friendly atmosphere proved their trademark. English Tea Time is usually from 3PM to 5PM and is typically served with tiny sandwiches, scones followed by sweets. Kids kept requesting the song "Blow the Man Down" and after continuous laughter from the British, they memorized the song and joined in with the chorus. "Wotcha" was a common greeting but "Talley-Ho" and "Right-Ho Chap" were some of the favorite slogans. The guests at the Irish Pub were truly jocose. (7) End of England's tour: It is a must to attend a stage play at the London Theatre. "Emperor's New Clothes" was scheduled our last night and the costumes "fit the bill". Missy was not impressed with the emperor's stage costume looking as if he did not have any clothes on…..and expressed herself to the audience. (Bill & George William laughed)

Leaving the Holiday Inn in London and soaking in the

sights before we board the ferry was a cheerful MEMORY.!
(Ref: Personal experiences with family.)

FRIENDLY HOLLAND: There are as many bikes as
people, in the Centre of Amsterdam, probably the most cycle-
friendly city in the world for its easy terrain and bicycle lanes.
Last account, Amsterdam had people from 170 nationalities.
English is widely spoken. Amsterdam is the capital whereas
the government body is located at The Hague. This populous
city of Holland/Netherlands is surrounded by colorful
homes, canals, and bridges therefore one of Europe's most
picturesque country. Sweet little ladies crocheting on the
streets is an aesthetic sight. Stereotypes about the Dutch
are usually associated with blond hair, blue eyes, and tall;
but they prefer to have Love, Pride, Workers, and accept all
nationalities. Amsterdam is intimately connected with water.
Its 165 canals were created over centuries to stimulate trade,
transport, and reclaim land to expand the city.

Canal cruises is one of the best ways to explore the city
with programmed destinations.

These guided boat trips offer unparalleled of centuries- old
architecture, canal houses and monuments, Skinny Bridge,
Amstel River and Hermitage Museum with other important
landmarks. (1) Former office of Dutch West India Company
(2) Oldest residence built in 1590 (3) Home of Rembrant who
lived and worked from 1639 to 1658. 17th Century painter and
etcher whose work came to dominate the Dutch Golden Ages.
Most famous painting was <u>Night Watch</u> which was the largest
painting of Rembrant's work with measurement of 142.9 in.
X 172.0 in. contrasting the light and dark in this military

portrait. Other popular paintings are: <u>Bathsheba and Her Bath</u> & <u>Stormy Sea of Galilee</u>. (4) Van Gogh Museum has the largest collection of work by Vincent Van Gogh in the world. This includes 200 paintings, 500 + drawings and 750 letters with landscapes, still life, portraits, and western art. <u>Starry Night</u> was one of his most famous painting characterizing bold colors and dramatic, impulsive and expressive brushwork that contributed to the modern era. Van Gogh committed suicide at the age of 37 came after years of mental illness and poverty. (5) Red Light District: Of course the kids noticed the red neon lights that displayed a charming area –but we did not explain prostitution. Amsterdam is today one of the most liberal cities in the world regarding sex and drugs. We geared them in a discussion about the history of Anne Frank and the Holocaust.

Anne Frank Museum: Holocaust was World War II genocide of European Jews. Between 1941 and 1945, across German occupied Europe Nazi Soldiers with order from Chancellor Adolph Hitler systematically murdered some six million Jews, around two-thirds of European Jewish population. The murders were carried out in mass shootings, extermination through concentration camps and gas chambers. Anne Frank's Diary proved to be a war document. Anne received her diary on her thirteenth birthday in 1942 and began documenting her war time experiences. Story of her family and friends hiding in the "secret annex" living out of sight in the middle of Amsterdam for two years and hiding from the persecution of Jews. She wrote about their protectors' efforts to smuggle in the essentials of life at a great risk. At fifteen, Anne was arrested, died of starvation and disease at the Bergen-Belsen concentration camp but her diary outlived her. Her most famous quote "in spite of everything, I still believe that people are really good at heart". Anne will live in our hearts forever! Good knowledge for our children.

Visit to Heineken Brewery: Heineken was first enjoyed in 1864, when 22-year old Gerard Heineken bought the old Amsterdam brewery dating from 1592, then called (The Haystack). Brewing ingredients are barley, hops (female flower), yeast, and water in large copper kettles is boiled and sieved until it becomes a honey colored solution called "wort"; and young beer ripens to freezing point which takes several weeks. The smell is not at all tempting. Of course, we were asked taste but kids and I declined and Bill passed his approval. U.S.A. is Heineken's biggest export market.

Touring Holland will always be a memorable beautiful scenery with over seven million tulip bulbs blooming in the Spring; and Dutch windmills is one of the most iconic symbols of the Netherlands. Windmills have played a vital role in their history pumping water and milling grain Today more than 1,000 windmills scattered through the country with many still in use.

Cannot leave Holland without the story of <u>The Little Boy That Saved Holland</u> but never lived. There was a leak in the dike (wall or dam to keep back a river) and the little boy stuck his finger in dike and the leak stopped. A Burgomaster Admiral told the little boy how brave he was and asked the council to make him a "hero". More leaks appeared and more boys volunteered for the mission; but the boys were exhausted! Finally the council decided to dig new beds for the North Sea. (Joke) This story was written by Mary Maples Dodge written in America and did not come from Holland.

ITALY

The ladies "clique" boarded a train in Brussels, Belgium to Florence, Italy. After acquiring our tickets, we had a few surprises! (Important emphasis on traveling with four ladies is more fun than winning the lottery) Mary, Pat, Grogan, and I were split into two sleeping cars. Mary & I were more or less "bunking" with a family of Italians who were supplied with wine and goat cheese; and of course it would have been rude if we did not accept their hospitality. They kept passing the goat cheese (strong with an unusual flavor) and I kept hiding it in my purse. After coming to our stop, we were a little dizzy with too much wine. We were told to bring as many KENNEDY HALF DOLLARS because Italians cherished Pres. Kennedy; and they proved to be a lifesaver tipping the cab, room service, restaurants, and shops usually discounted the price for a Kennedy Half Dollar.

Our main goal was to "shop until we dropped" in Florence, Italy. We bought enough leather goods for Christmas presents to give our families for a number of years; and bought enough shoes to open a store; only being four sizes but different colors and styles. Who can leave Italy without Florentine items and alabaster items even though packing was a problem?

Our only tour was to observe the Leaning Tower of Pisa. The bell tower was not originally meant to lean- because it was built on loose soil the tower gradually lifted to one side. This tower is becoming an icon in Italy.

We did not make it to Vatican City State but regretted after trip was over. Hoping Pope Paul VI understands "running out of money" but we definitely helped the economy in Italy.

Shopping in France and England with the girls: We rode a train to Paris and shopped in expensive stores but not much purchasing. Food was excellent-especially the moules-frites, lobster, clam, and crab.

Riding a ferry to England but spending time in their pubs was an excellent gesture of meeting the British. They loved Mary who was a good beer or ale drinker because she toasted every glass to them. Mary was always the "laugh of any party".

Back to the story: President Nixon served as the 37th President from 1969-1974 but his scandal did not help the American Troops in Belgium. The only President to resign only to face almost certain impeachment and removal from office on August 9, 1974. ("Watergate Scandal") Charges were burglary by five men of Democratic party; Nixon's administrators bugged offices and Nixon tried to illegally cover the activities. He was succeeded by President Ford. Our tour of duty in Belgium was 1972-1976. During this tour, I taught for the Dept. of Defense in an international school. Teaching 149 5th graders was a challenge each day; but part of their curriculum was to travel to Switzerland and learn to ski, tour the Swiss Alps and have a good knowledge of their culture. One half day was scheduled for teaching, and the other half was for skiing, touring, and meeting the Swiss people. So the students, four female parents, and myself boarded a train from Brussels then switched to a cog railroad being important part of infrastructure helping to access the high alpine environment and enjoy the breathtaking scenery of the highest peaks of Switzerland. I had the task of chaperoning the boys and we had our daily meeting each morning on rules, manners, consequences on behavior, health, sickness, home sick, and of course a daily prayer knowing I needed it more than the boys. I talked with them about eating the correct foods, personal hygiene, and always let me know of any kind of problem which included regular trips to bathroom. In order not to embarrass this personal problem, at the beginning of each meeting to nod their head if there was a problem. About two days in the trip, Tim-0 (sweet student) nodded his head. In private we contacted the nurse in the hotel and medication was prescribed. Next day at the early meeting, Tim-O nodded his head again. We went back to nurse and she doubled the medication. The next day a field trip was planned and I strongly advised Tim-O to stay at the hotel. He convinced me he would be o.k. About half way of field trip on that snowy mountain without even a small tree in sight, I heard this mournful cry of "Ms. Joyce" Help. I told the boys to form a circle around him and he took care of business. . He was a good sport and the way back to hotel-we all had a good laugh especially the guys.

Back to Belgium: Seems everything was going well with kids making good grades; Bill flying the helicopter; Mary and I shopping at the flea markets buying treasures. BUT an event caused the family to be sad; Sam our lovable dachshund would turnover a colonel's trash can who must have had good smelling leftover food. The colonel pressed charges and we had to send Sam back to the states; being a tearful morning for us. PaPaw (Keeper) checked the airlines, but Sam was lost. They traced him back to Chicago and they immediately put him on a plane to San Angelo, Texas. (For those who are animals lovers would understand)

Leaving Belgium with stored knowledge of Europe and the cultures will always be good memories but being anxious to see family and being able to love Sam (dog) was more exciting.

Another Leg: Ft. Hood, Texas (1976-1984)

We bought a home in Lampasas, Texas and kids entered Jr. High and High School. Missy was very good with the baton and became a majorette for the Junior High School; and in High school being a part of the drill team, tennis, and basketball team. George Wm. continued his talent in baseball and was selected to All-State student from Lampasas with a recognition program in Austin, Texas. Bill volunteered for a military tour in Korea for two years; and this was the beginning of a sad emotional storm. George William was working for a rancher building feed containers for the animals; and a nail broke and hit him in the eye. His friend, Mark took him to hospital but Dr. Brooks ordered a helicopter to rush him to Scott/White Hospital in Temple. Mother and Daddy were there at my side waiting for the news after a four hr. surgery. News was not good and there have been complications to this date concerning his eyesight.

Teaching 8th grade history in Lampasas proved to open more doors for me. Planning a History Fair for the students was successful and being part of Texas Historical Association with students winning awards in Texas.

The committee of "Spring Ho" (annual event in Lampasas) selected yours truly to be a part of planning for events. This committee became my closest friends serving three years. Of course my teaching buddies and bridge club deserves a plus.

Bill had problems with alcohol and drinking on the road. It was a constant worry hoping he would not have a wreck or hurt someone. I tried to drink strong bourbon with him but it always made me sick. We attended counseling sessions proving unsuccessful but church helped to bring temporary peace. Buying a boat for the kids to ski was a positive move with daily camping trips at Inks Lake near Lampasas. Drinking will ruin a marriage but more important it puts a strain on the children. Bill filed for divorce thinking it would solve the problem; but it backfired and brought more problems on our kids. George Wm. enrolled at Angelo State University living with Bill's parents. Missy and I continued to live in our home until she finished high school. Whenever she was accepted at A & M, I knew I would have to move because of financial obligations. Worry with emotional stress became an issue and Dr. Brooks put me in hospital. God sent a navigator (Dr. Brooks) and told me I had two choices: (1) Stay in bed and feel sorry for yourself or (2) Get busy with your life—which I chose to do! Missy encouraged me to apply with Dept. of Defense again with welcoming orders to teach Social Studies in Yongsan, Korea at Seoul American School. (Personal stories from Author)

KOREA: 1984-1986

Korea is a region in East Asia and since 1948 it has been divided between two distinct states: North Korea and South Korea. The history began at the end of World War II in 1945. The surrender of Japan led to the division of Korea at the 38th parallel with Soviet Union occupying the North and United States occupying the South. U.S. and Soviet Union failed to agree on a way to unify the country, and in 1948 they established separate governments, called the DMZ (Korean Demilitarized Zone).

Rice production in South Korea is necessary for food supply with rice being part of their diet. Annually- rice production was usually measured in tons instead of pounds. Ladies use rice water for a smooth complexion and they need it after working for hours in the fields.

Kimchi cuisine is a famous traditional side dish of fermented vegetables-cabbage and radishes cooked with a variety of spices with plenty of garlic and ginger. One allows kimchi to ferment for up to five days in a glass jar (Some Koreans use their rooftops); and then five days in the refrigerator. The Koreans believe kimchi prevents cancer and digestive problems with other health benefits.

A popular TV show "M.A.S.H." must be mentioned about the Korean War to deal with medical situations with laughter in a Military Hospital located in Korea. Mobile Army Surgical Hospital units were to treat a wounded soldier as quickly as possible with units located close to front line.

The unexpected challenges and becoming independent in this small country was the "right medicine" during this time in my life. Teaching Social Studies at Yongsan Military base in Seoul was a "joy" with well-behaved students. These young people's views were positive and knew if they misbehaved, "Father was called and that did not set well with the military".. The students needed a Student Council sponsor as they approached me with sad eyes and determination. The only major dilemma during this sponsorship were the students taking the crystals from the chandeliers at the Junior & Senior Prom which was located at a five star hotel in the center of Seoul. I was naïve not noticing the girls wearing the crystals as earrings. The hotel owner called our superintendent the next day and stated we were responsible for the chandelier; after posting a letter in our school newspaper the students were told to put the crystals on my desk the next morning. They were accountable with all the crystals neatly spread on my desk; but also having a good laugh pulling wool over their sponsor's eyes.) Typical students looking for fun and realizing they went too far.

Having a soft spot in my heart for young people kept me busy! The high school wrestling team also needed a sponsor creating another extracurricular job. Being responsible for paperwork, reserving hotels and locating good restaurants was my main priority but travel plans to Japan, Philippines, and major cities in Korea kept one busy besides trying to be a "good Mom" for them. I did not know one rule about wrestling but learned quickly thanks to a good coach. Strong-willed with determination, excellent sportsmanship, smart, and respect for their opponents are few of the reasons several young men from wrestling team were selected for West Point.

"A Little Bit of History Never Hurt Anyone" was a play of U.S. Presidents and First Ladies of my History Class. I knew if help was needed on their costumes portraying their characters; they could easily find their costumes in Itaewon, a popular shopping center in Seoul. My students were dressed to perfection giving historical remarks about their character. The auditorium was packed with standing applauses singing "This Land Is Your Land" which would have made Guthrie (composer) and the popular Bruce Springsteen proud. Of course, each student received an "A" for their performance mainly because of their laborious job.

Our principal was a kind considerate Christian that devoted his life to Department of Defense in the Education field and always protecting his students. It seemed a young girl was abused at home and needed someone to take care of her for six weeks until she was transferred back to states. He contacted the right person and she adjusted to our friendship with always a smile. Our bonding began watching the structures of 1988 Olympic on a daily basis for four weeks. .Two goals were completed: Respect and love for one another and of course the History of Olympics in Seoul Korea.

Challenger Shuttle: Teachers could apply for this mission and passing one to five but failing six and seven requirements disqualified me. On January 28, 1986, 73 seconds after takeoff the shuttle erupted in a fireball and the entire crew was killed. Mother was diagnosed with cancer during my assignment and I will always remember the last telephone call from her stating: "I am so glad you failed part of test."

Meeting my best friend, Jim, in Korea was compared to a falling star! He always knew what to do, what to say, and made me feel I was special. Besides touring the DMZ together; we were never bored looking for historical sites, traveling to islands, sampling unusual food, shopping at the market and always with positive outlook on life without stress. Sadly, Jim was killed in an airplane crash but his memory will always be a part of my life.

Missy (daughter) being a minor was allowed to come to Korea and we took advantage of shopping, traveling to Hong Kong, and completing the trip in Hawaii. Jackie and Midge (friends) also made a visit to Korea and every day they could not wait to shop-shop! Highlight of Thanksgiving 1985 was visiting the troops in a remote site near the mountains of North Korea. My neighbor who was a General in Officer's BQ, planned the trip and appointed a nice colonel to be may guide. Traveling by helicopter to the hills that separated South Korea from North Korea was sad sight but meeting the men and women stationed in this remote area was appreciative. Bless these men and women of the military who continuously protect our lives in every part of the world.

Mary (friend) and I reserved a free passage to Philippines on an old WWII plane. We hired a guide to take us to the best places but spending too much money put the "broke girls" in a bad situation. We spent too much money on wooden dishes and furniture. The plane on return trip to Korea had an engine problem and we were forced to land in Japan. We were given a room but not enough money for food. Mary contacted Dick to send money so we survived and landing in Korea with Dick shaking his head brought laughter of our adventure.

March, 1986, an emergency call was received to come home to say good bye to my Mother. She was brave, thoughtful, loved her family, never feeling sorry for herself with her sickness and always saying "someone else is suffering more than me". Being the best working Mother in world taking care of six kids and husband; she earned the right to be put on a pedestal. Mother died on March 31, 1986 of lung cancer at the young age of 68. With Daddy being alone, I spoke to our principal about returning home and being the kind principal he understood. The Koreans, students, and friends at Yongsan Military Base renewed my faith with gratitude working in Korea; and knowing that I will never forget my energetic high school students. A precious historical sight were children (ages three-to five) marching in school uniforms but always peeping over their shoulders to view the Americans with a smile.

Back to Texas: Helping Daddy was easy—if the meal was on table at 12:00 P.M, supper at 6:00 P.M., Wheel of Fortune at 6:30 P.M. and his bedtime at 9:00 P.M. Big Ranch was his salvation and I was elected to open and close gates. Many times we had to haul water and take care of sick sheep but there was no problem with this ole rancher. Since Daddy remarried, a door opened again. My friend, Pete had lost his wife from cancer and needed help with his two teen-age girls. Living in Houston, Texas was an enormous change from the country. Sweet girls were in a private school and of course losing their Mother put a strain on their lives but we survived with few problems. They never demanded anything and was always appreciative of home cooked meals, clean laundry, and a shoulder to cry on as needed. Pete found a "nanny" for the girls and helping out in an emergency gives one a good feeling of being a good friend.

: Pete encouraged me to complete my Master's Degree in Counseling. There was a job opening for a Social Studies teacher in Uvalde, Texas so packing my belongings, accepting the job, and enrolling in graduate school at Sul Ross University for night classes. Two years later, I completed my Master's in counseling. To celebrate, some fun trips were planned with Mother's two sisters Aunt Opal, Aunt Jo, and a niece, sweet Helen. Helen and I took them to Las Vegas attending several shows, and the best show were the guys dressing as ladies and modeling. Aunt Jo and Aunt Opal kept watching them and stated "they are pretty girls but need to lose some weight"; Helen and I could not stop laughing after we told them they were men. Aunt Opal played the slots and after her four quarters were gone-she did not play anymore saying "I am not going to throw my hard earned money away." The last trips included Branson, Nashville with Grand Ole Opry, and Disney World and I know Mother would have been proud and only wishing she was with us.

MOVING BACK
TO WEST TEXAS

Accepting a position as Elementary and Jr. High counselor of over 300 students in Coleman, Texas was another blessing of helping children and young people. Coleman was only 25 miles to Big Ranch and Daddy could depend upon me for help. Living in an old funeral home was interesting with the embalming room in the utility room. My young nieces and nephews claimed they could hear strange noises at night .

The most unusual cases were sending young boys to West Texas Boy's Ranch since parents had financial problems and were not being able to care properly for the boys. These young boys did fine especially one boy that would always visit during the summer. Abuse cases, truancy, stealing, academic failure, fighting, and one young student dying from leukemia requiring support with home visits; but always with a listening ear to help the confused students with a positive attitude. Deciding to build a house in the country was a good idea but created some major problems. The builder after a signed contract took me to court saying he misjudged the price; and proving this was in very small font on the last page of contract "estimate plus". The jury did not take into consideration of

Daddy and I bringing all the rocks from the big ranch for the exterior of home, pouring cement for the driveway, paying for hot tub; and regular cleaning after the carpenters left for the day. The jury ruled that $10,000.00 should be paid to the builder. The presiding judge agreed with me and told me to put this behind me and go forward. I did not have $10,000.00- so I applied for a job in ALASKA. I turned my disappointment into a blessing being an itinerant counselor for Alaskan rural schools. The natives and chiefs of Alaska taught yours truly the value of the tribes and traditions one could only learn in their frontier. "one must earn their trust in Alaska".

North to Alaska: Alaska is an U.S. state in NE extremity of US west coast, just across the Bering Strait from Asia with Canadian territories of British Columbia and territory of Yukon borders to the east and southeast. Alaska was acquired in 1867, territory was dubbed as "Seward's Folly" after Secretary of State Seward arranged to buy it from Russia for 7.2 million and today it would be valued over 105 million. Discovery of gold in 1890's created a stampede of prospectors and settlers. Population is approximately 739,795 in 1992 with 586,400 square miles and Juneau being the capital. Economy is dominated by fishing, natural gas, and oil industries in abundance thanks to the Alaskan Pipeline. Salmon fishing is popular sport but also home to crustaceans, variety of different fish, seals, sea lions, and whales living in seas, lakes, and rivers.

Three types of bear reign in Alaska: Black Bear, Brown Bear, and Polar Bear. Moose dominates most areas; Bison, Mountain goats, and migration of caribou traveling about

2,400 KM to birthing grounds. Bald Eagle along with 430 species of birds; cannot forget the two types of turtles: Green and Leatherback. Alaska is home to 7,000-11,000 wolves.

Annual Iditarod is a Sled Dog Race from Anchorage all the way to Nome on the western coast of Bering Strait with an area of 1,100 miles. Historical trail begins the first Saturday in March which celebrates the legacy of the mushers and their devoted breeds of Siberians Huskies and Alaskan Malamutes. The Area covers a length of 1,100 miles within 8-15 days. Interesting sled dog vocabulary: Hike-Let's Go, Haw-Turn left, Gee-Turn right, On by- Overtake, Easy-Slowdown, Whoa-Stop.

Being employed by Yukon Koyukuk School District and being responsible for five rural schools with bush planes for transportation was a daily routine with unexpected surprises.. Bush pilots: Lower 48 could learn from the skilled bush pilots in Alaska flying below zero temperature. Number #1 priority before you fly is to purchase the proper gear such as a heavy parka, leather gloves, silk long johns with ski pants, warm cap, and using layers of tops with a sweater. Once in the cockpit the pilot explains the emergency gear and information on emergency landing. Pilots share wisdom, experiences, and tall tales with their planes equipped with large tires, floats, and skis because of the rough terrain and snow making it easier to land or water if there is not landing strips or flying to remote areas. These friendly bush pilots deserve an annual salary of $58,963.00 to $102, 953.00. Working with students in Allakaket, Bettles, Manley, Minto, and Northwest was challenging and educational.. Bush planes would fly me to various schools on Monday and return Friday to my small apartment in Fairbanks; but sometimes being "snowed in" was not unusual. There is a high rate of suicides among teen-agers, drug and alcohol abuse, child abuse, FAS (Fetal Alcohol Syn.) teen-age pregnancies plus working very closely with the High School Seniors for careers and enrollment in colleges.

Allakaket was my first rural site. (1991) The village is on a river with approximately 200 Natives and the school enrollment were friendly willing 38 students accepting help as needed especially for drinking and truancy. Many home visits were scheduled with the parents. I slept in the schools with a couch for my bedroll, running water, a public bathroom, and a small kitchen with microwave. I had to pack light and carried dozens of Nissin Cup Noodles with me but usually was invited to different homes for dinner experiencing the different ways of cooking moose and salmon. There are no cars but Four-wheelers, numerous snow-mobiles, and most families have six to eight dogs using them for sleds but many nights they howled constantly because of the wolves. Jarrod, a six year old living with a grandparent, became my guide with the knowledge of traditions in Alaska. Jarrod introduced me to a 91 year old chief that gladly supplied my curious knowledge of traditions in Alaska. (1) Bear Party: Only men can attend after a successful hunt stating if they allow women to attend the spirits will not be good and besides the woman's hair will turn white and be mean. (2) Natives believed that both humans and animals have souls and trees, mountains, rivers, sun, moon, stars have spirits. One must treat nature with respect and never say "I am going hunting" always say "I am going to look around" to protect the spirits. (3)A bear skin was thought to hate death and would therefore drive the sickness out of a person who lay on the skin. (4) Charms were used to ward off danger or brought good fortune. (5) Respect the Medicine Man because he heals sickness and interprets messages from the spirit world. (6) The animal eyes were usually cut out first because the spirit is still around and if eyes are gone they will not see the dressing process. (7) The chief did explain the potlatch and attending one in Minto helped me to understand the purpose. (8) Outsiders are accepted by the village if approved by the chief and I did meet their standards receiving a pair of beaded moccasins. (9) Daylight hours occur between May 17 through July 27. Midnight sun or dark days from middle of November to end of January. (Chief explained that is the time to keep a close eye on your children) Jarred asked the chief if his son could take us to look around and fish. So the chief's son, Jarrod and I left on a flatboat down the river in the late evening. We stopped because he had spotted a moose but Jarred and I had to stay on the river bank. We decided to fish with Jarred throwing out his line and giving the pole to me. Then like a blink of an eye I felt as if something was trying to pull me in river. Jarred kept saying to keep line straight in order for him to club it. I tried but the fish got away with lure and of course broke the line. Jarrod stating firmly if you would had listen to me-we would have fish for supper. The fish was a sheefish and the normal size is about four feet long. Six year old Jarred was not only a hunter but an expert fisherman. The chief's son did kill a moose so the trip was successful. The chief told me I brought Good Luck and Jarred and I had fish stories to tell to his class. Jarred was always the first to meet the bush plane bringing the snowmobile whenever I landed in Allakaket but with parents' permission my little Natives were on the roof waving as the plane descended in their village. The average gage showed 123.7 inches from September to January, 1990. Usually the adults were on rooftops shoveling snow because heavy snow can cause serious damage to their log cabins. In April the snow begins to melt and can cause problems with flooding because of the many rivers (Koyukuk and Old Man River) and lakes.

Minto Village: (1990) Minto had a population around 300 with 74 students being my largest rural school. The students are very athletic and participate in basketball and cross-country skiing. They are given many opportunities to participate in extra-curricular activities. Ski Meets are held during the winter months inviting other schools to participate in Minto. Young skiers follow a course with their guns. At the end of the course, they have a target to shoot with five bullets. If they miss the target they must start the course again because in order to win one must hit target 5 out of 5 and only have 3 chances. Skis are like shoes to them; and the gun is important since they are in the wilderness so much. A 11-year old boy taught me how to wear snowshoes in order to make accurate records with the contestants. This young boy was amazing on the skis and as usual had a special place in my heart. He decided to come to Texas and live with me since his Mother was an alcoholic and his grandmother was sick. State was going to put him in Foster Home but a family member adopted him knowing he would not be happy in "hot Texas". The young people get-along well with each other and if one student is ugly to another- watch out! Interesting case was a mature 17 yr. senior inquiring how to apply for the Job Corp and we researched the qualifications. Job Corp is a no cost education and training administered by U.S. Dept. of Labor that helps young people ages 16-24 improve the quality of their lives of empowering them to great jobs and become independent. After graduation he was ready to go. Observing young people gives a clue to their behavior and I knew a young pretty girl had worries, and I made it a point to smile daily at her knowing she needed to talk. An elderly man died in the village being a relative...she came and stated she did not care because of the abuse than lasted for years. We had regular sessions and eventually she was relieved of any guilt. After returning to Texas I received a graduation announcement from a modeling school with her picture wearing a beautiful engagement ring and smiling. A high school student committed suicide on the frozen lakes by drinking too much. The villages hold potlatches which is a gathering of people whenever someone dies. It is called a potlatch because one is expected to go to community hall and family of deceased serves everyone. If you do not attend- then you are not respected. Everyone sits in a huge circle and butcher paper is rolled out and family brings moose soup, moose and caribou, salads, and ice cream made with fat from a caribou. You accept everything they give you and if you deny anything that is an insult to the family. If you bring a covered dish one is saved because you can take home what you do not eat. The family serves you because they feel if they are busy there is no time to mourn. Meals and Native Dancing are nightly and after the funeral the last potlatch completes the ritual. (experiences in Alaska).

The Minto students encouraged me to hike to a mountain

and view the Northern Lights (Alaska Aurora Borealis).We had the best seat in the house watching the glimmering ribbons of color that flash across the sky. One student explained the colors are formed when sun's particles interact with nitrogen. The colors are determined by gases in the Earth's atmosphere and incoming solar particles tend to collide with different gases at different heights. He also stated the Vikings thought the lights were caused by shining weapons of immortal soldiers; and certain tribes of Alaska believed the lights were the souls of salmon, deer, and many other animals. Hours later it was time to return to village but I know one young student will be successful in whatever occupation he chooses.

Experiencing my first earthquake was in Minto sleeping in my bedroll. I woke noticing the furniture was moving and lights were shaking with strange noises. Did not last very long and afterwards the principal checked on me and said it was a mild earthquake. It was safe to go back to sleep. HELLO!

My high school students and I attended a wolf summit featuring 93 year old Native Peter John, Governor of Alaska, and assigned government delegates. The Alaskan Natives wanted to control the number of wolves that would be killed because the wolves would kill the moose and caused a shortage in their food supply. The delegates wanted to protect the wolves but a compromise was made in reference of protecting the food supply. Alaskans should be the lawmakers of their state.

Manley(1992) Leaving Minto and flying to Manley Hot Springs: The population of this village is 100 and the school enrollment is 22. The school is modern equipped with a computer for each child. The students were involved with a

Reading Program called "Battle of Books" and received neat prizes for reading and answering questions. Listening to a student read created an opportunity to have an individual conversation with trust and becoming acquainted with counselor. "Battle of Books" competition uses telephone and computer to "battle" with other villages and students win grand prizes as winners.

The small village is aware of newcomers relating to a tragedy in 1983. A veteran of Viet Nam War rented an old hunter's cabin close to the river; whenever residents would watch the "ice cracking" and one day residents noticed the cars parked but no owners (Cars can drive from Fairbanks to Manley- if you are an experienced driver.) State troopers were called and this man had killed 7 people that day and threw the bodies in the river. (Pregnant Mother, two year old son, and husband; man with cerebral palsy; husband and wife; and a young minister.) The troopers located him from a helicopter and before they could land-he shot the helicopter and killed a state trooper. The other troopers opened fire and killed him. Sad history of this small village.

Flying from Manley to Fairbanks with temperatures below 50 degrees. Being snowbound in Manley for two weeks but hoping I would make connections to fly home for Christmas. Bush Pilots are not allowed to fly if temperature is less than 45 degrees below. Since pilot knew I had a ticket to Texas for Christmas and observing 43 degrees below he told me to board his plane. Crossing a mountain on our journey we experienced an "ice fog" causing the pilot to have visual problems. The bush pilot looked at me and asked, "Joyce, do you know where survival gear is located?" I looked at his strained face, said yes, and asked him "Are we were going to die?". He said "it's possible" but we had another pilot in the clouds that guided us safely to Fairbanks.

Flying to Bettles: (1991) The bush pilot recommended a detour to the Arctic Circle before landing at the school in Bettles. Taking the route to Anaktuvik Pass in the Brooks Range area of Alaska and crossing the Arctic National Park of home to Nunamiut Eskimos was truly God's beautiful creations. The caribou migration of approximately 164,000 was spotted from the plane; migration is considered one of the most wildlife impressive phenomenon in this part of the world. They travel about 400-500 miles to find food and live on fat for rotting purposes. Truly one of the highlights of Alaska!

BettlesL1991) The village has a population of 52 with 8 students. Tourists and hunters occupy the community lodge during hunting seasons and are allowed to drive on the frozen rivers if temperature is below 50 degrees. The students are very fortunate to have the following facilities: fabulous library, T.V. room with videos, computer room, sewing room, science lab, gym, and classrooms. The students were always anxious to converse on their life at this small village with survival techniques; and a snow mobile was used to have parent conferences in their home. These young students used their skills to enjoy their life in the isolated village. At night, students & I would take a glass of water and at the count of three, we would throw the water upward and the winner would be the water that froze first. Teaching the skills of dog mushing and ice skating were definite challenges but students help me to succeed. The fun times were also bonding time with few student problems.

Northwinds: These are students that live in remote rural areas and are enrolled in school by correspondence courses. Teachers visit them monthly and if there is an emotional problem, the school district assigns me to fly to the remote area. Encountering only two major problems during my employment: (1) One of my 17 yr. old native had a warrant for his arrest and persuading the State Patrol to set community work schedule for him was acceptable with probation. He was as tough as nails and I told him it was not the bears turning my hair grey- it was him. After several visits, he did calm down and always had a funny remark about my hair. (2) An angry 8 yr. old boy with a single dad was killing dogs after his Mother had died. The district recommended some psychiatric care in Fairbanks and we left in the bush plane. Time and counseling helped and eventually the young boy was returned home with regular visits.

Juneau: The Alaskan Student Government conference was held in the capital and could only reach Juneau by plane. Seven Native boys and girls were selected from my schools with around 500 students from different areas of Alaska. The students planned the entire conference and adults were very impressed of their organizational skills. Educational Field trips were scheduled : Capital Building, Governor's Mansion, Old gold mines, Mendenhall Glacier formed during the ice age which began 3,000 years ago and the striking feature is its blue color, museums, and students specially enjoyed the Gastineau Salmon Hatchery relating to the spawning process releasing over 150 million of pink and chum salmon. The annual rainfall is 99 inches causing good fishing, sights of humpback whales, harbor seals, and sea lions. We attended a Presbyterian Church called Chapel by the Lake because one wall was completely glass viewing a glacier, mountains, lake, and trees. GOD did Good! (Alaskan History)

Daddy and two friends (Era & Jackie) arrived in Alaska in the month of May. Daddy especially enjoyed his flight on a bush plane to Nome, Alaska viewing the scenery and animals but riding on a train in Denali National Park was a lifetime experience. It was time to go home but leaving the Last Frontier will always be heartwarming experiences of the friendships of the natives, beauty of Alaska with wildlife, and the many educational opportunities of working in this beautiful state. Another journey with blessings from GOD. Saved $10,000.00 for my Texas home by sleeping in the schools, bringing dry soups for lunch, and dinner invitations from Natives; but enjoying free time attending the Olympic Ice Sculpturing contests, Ice Hockey Games, and playing games with the children. Jackie, friend, volunteered to help me drive the Canadian Route to Texas. Our first stop was in Chicken, Alaska before we entered Dalton Highway. This very small town had a population of 7 with a post office, café, saloon, and two outhouses. Chicken was founded on gold seekers and still surviving wishing for a gold strike. Canada was nearly as beautiful as Alaska with beautiful mountains and wild life, but entering the lower 48 to the state of Texas was home.

LIL RANCH IN TEXAS

God's creation of Alaska was unbelievable, and the first view of my Lil Ranch was thanking the Good Lord for an incredible journey but ready to homestead. The Lil Ranch needed animals so it was time for adoption. Daddy brought goats with a leader (Hercules) and included Molly Bee with three babies, friend gave me a donkey (Matilda) living 38 years on the Lil Ranch, three llamas (Willie, Dolly Llama, Sweetie), Miniature African sheep (Prissy), pot-bellied pig named Daisy Mae, one chicken (Donnie Mae), two geese (Henry and Henrietta), two ducks (Dick & Jane), Rooster Cockburn, two peacock (Pete & Patricia), miniature pony (Polly), wild mustang adopted from an auction(Sally), five cats, (Barney, Miss Kitty, Kolby, Tiger, Tripod), One Fine dog, (Border collie named Max), three spoiled dachshunds (Katy, BoJo, Pedro). The animal cemetery is filled with good thoughts of those who have passed away. Besides the critters, deer, wild turkey, and squirrels, enjoy the leftovers but very cautious of strangers. Wild pigs are a nuisance damaging fences; coyotes are never welcomed howling at night waiting to kill their harmless prey. School students always enjoyed coming to Lil Ranch for their field trips and the critters always welcomed them.

Accepting a position as counselor in Brownwood, Texas for K-3rd grades keeping busy with these young children because they always listened with respect. Daddy was in an accident due to 18wheeler truck hitting him being hospitalized for several months with brain damage; afterwards home care was on a regular basis of 24 hours with each caregiver working 8 hours. I interviewed for a counselor's position in Ballinger in order to help in any way for Daddy. Ballinger ISD in Texas was rated well and enjoyed every working hour with the students from K-5th grades, considerate principal, and super teachers. Checking on Daddy every day gave me a sense of satisfaction of love and respect for him. 9-11-2001 was a terrible time in history due to Islamic terrorists attacking the United States killing 2,977 people.. Trying to explain this sad event confused him like the rest of Americans and asking if Hitler had a part in it. Daddy died February 9, 2002 but will always be remembered as a quiet man with gifts of charity and knowledge of the world with his own ideas. Sometimes, a little stubborn and Mother deserved a gold star for keeping him in line.

Job description in Ballinger was comparable to my other positions: Individual and group counseling, truancy, academic grades, working with Child Welfare, class presentations, Texas Tests, career day, and the list goes on…. Sad case was a young boy committing suicide and grieving groups were scheduled for his friends. Ballinger staff at BISD was comparable to a family; we worked closely together even on fun trips with young teachers named Darlene and Christy who became true friends.

Every counselor has a funny story to share: Living at the Lil Ranch and commuting to work usually took an hour.

Therefore I always left a chair in front of my office if a student needed to talk before I arrived at school. As I turned the hall corner, an elementary student was sitting in the chair. He immediately stated "Ms. Joyce, I need to talk to you"! Being an honor student, I knew this could be serious. Asking him if I could pour my cup of coffee and the answer was if you hurry; but we must close the door. I sat down at my desk and he pulled a chair beside me and asked him if there was a problem. He looked at me with trust, and asked: "Ms. Joyce, why are there sex problems in Washington .D.C.? I think coffee flew everywhere and wished I could have disappeared at that moment. I asked him if he had talked to his parents and he stated, "they told me to ask you". I called his Mother and told her this situation: "Please Ms. Joyce, talk to him". Explaining this sex question was difficult on a young elementary level but he was satisfied with the simple answer without too much detail. The following day coming to my office, I was thinking about the chair and hoping to solve any problem. Walking into my office was a beautiful bouquet of flowers with a "Thank You Note" attached. Calling parent to acknowledge the flowers, it was suggested if a child has a question he/she needs an answer. Media can confuse our children relating to presidents.

Time to retire with 32 years of service! Missing the kids, I decided to volunteer with C.A.S.A., mentor to school students for academic reasons, and teaching Sunday School Classes. BUT being able to volunteer with Operation Smile was another highlight in my life. One morning listening to Dr. Schuller interviewing a guest on TV from Operation Smile explained the need for anyone to volunteer with this charitable program.

Operation Smile travels to many developing countries to operate on children with medical problems particularly cleft lips and palates. The skilled volunteers of medical professional field give their time and love to these children. Working with the volunteers,, parents of children, loving the children, respecting their country and cultures, touring the countryside fulfilled my continuous love for children. I truly will always be grateful to OPERATION SMILE for permitting me to be a part of a child's life.

MOTHER TERESA:

"PEACE BEGINS WITH A SMILE"

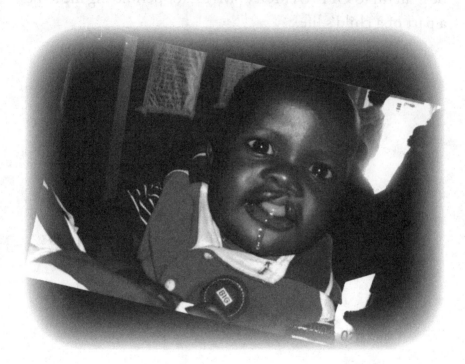

OPERATION SMILE: Throughout the world, Operation Smile volunteers repair childhood facial deformities. In 1982, Dr. Magee, a plastic surgeon and his wife, Kathy, a registered nurse, traveled to Philippines with a group of medical volunteers to repair children's cleft lip and cleft palates and discovered hundreds of children ravaged by deformities. As they prepared to leave the Philippines, they promised to return and this was the beginning of world wide Operation Smile. Operation Smile was born and over 28 countries with over 3,775 medical professionals from 57 countries filled 6,024 positions and donated 414,624 hours of time. Thousands of volunteers from around the world have performed surgery on 270,000 patients and more with 21,000 patients have receiving dental care. AND we are thankful to Dr. Magee and his wife Kathy for committing their lives to this organization. Mission Statement: Kathy and Dr. Magee stated, "Throughout the world, Operation Smile volunteers repair childhood facial deformities while building public and private partnerships that advocate healthcare systems for children and families. Together we create smiles, change lives, and humanity. Operation Smile builds a legacy of trust, hope, health and dignity for children hoping for a chance for a better life.

A cleft lip may be accompanied by an opening in the bones of the upper jaw or upper gum. A cleft palate occurs when the two sides of a palate do not join together, resulting in an opening in the roof of the mouth. The exact cause of a cleft is unknown. Cleft lips and cleft palates are congenital defects that occur in embryonic development. Scientists believe a combination of genetic and environmental factors, such as maternal illness, drugs or malnutrition, may lead to a cleft lip or cleft palate. Mothers who take multivitamins containing folic acid before conception and the first two months of pregnancy may reduce their risk of giving birth to a baby with cleft. Cleft lip or cleft palate can cause problems for the child: Ear disease and dental problems, speech development, and difficulty eating. These children are often teased or bullied about their condition which can cause low esteem. (Newsletter of Operation Smile/spokesman for Operation Smile)

First mission: AFRICA is the second largest of 11.7 million square miles and most populated continent with 1.29 billion as of 1918. It accounts for about 16% of world's human population. Africa is considered by most paleoanthropologists the oldest inhabited territory on earth. Although it has natural resources, Africa remains the world's poorest and least developed continent, the result of a variety of causes that may include a corrupt government that have often committed serious human rights violations, high level of illiteracy, lack of access to a foreign capital and military conflict (ranging from guerrilla warfare to genocide.

Poverty, illiteracy, malnutrition, and inadequate water

supply and sanitation, as well as poor health affect a large proportion of the people residing in Africa's continent.

Leaving Abilene, Texas on an early Tuesday morning with the longest layover in Amsterdam for 8 hrs. and the flight took 48 hours before landing in Nairobi, Africa. Arriving in Africa with a welcoming party of Africans verbalizing "Karibou" meaning "welcome", "Asante" meaning "Thank you" and "Jambo" meaning "hello" and always with a long handshake. The colorful costumes in the airport created a fashion show with friendly smiles and thanking us for helping their children "smile again". The volunteers boarded another plane to Kisumu and we had reservations at a small hotel with no air conditioners, no T.V. but was issued a net for our bed with a spray to keep mosquitos away. Since we were near Lake Victoria, the musical sound of frogs croaking all night was better than a sleeping pill.

Thirty people were on the team: Surgeons, anesthesiologists, dentist, childhood specialist, speech therapist, nurses from different countries, medical records, high school students, and interpreters, and a mission coordinator. The first staff meeting was 5AM giving us information for the mission. (1) Do not eat fresh vegetables that have not been cooked or boiled (2) Only drink bottled water and brush teeth with bottled water (3) Hot tea with hot milk will give one an energy lift since the working hours are normally 10-12 hours. (4) Breakfast is usually pork and beans. (5) Lunch: Red beans and rice which was cooked in a large iron pot making it very tasteful. (6) Vaccinations: Yellow fever vaccine is mandatory. Malaria is common and one must take doxycycline during your time in Kisumu and four weeks after you return home.

Other important vaccinations are: Hepatitis A and B, meningitis, typhoid, polio, tetanus, diphtheria, and measles. (7) Pay attention to mosquito protection between dusk and dawn because this is when the type of mosquito whose bite transmits malaria is active. (8) Use insect repellent that contains DEET. (9) Always sleep under a net and spray room. (10) During the day-wear long sleeved shirts, long pants, and a hat for protection.

Mission : Traveling to hospital at 5 A.M. was a tour on its own watching the people go to work and setting their vegetable booths with rows of colorful clothes. We had to check-in with the gatekeeper who wore an unusual hat which I complimented- did not know at the time this would bring a funny story whenever we left Africa. Our first chore was to clean the operating room and help the doctors and nurses with their screening booths. JoJo (surgeon from Philippines) was my mentor and made sure I understood the screening process for the children: (1) Medical Records (Joyce) with help of interpreters gained as much information on child/ parents relating to surgery and the age of child was very important for application. The parents with their child would walk two or three hours for the service and wait another two or three hours to be screened and never complained. (2) Speech therapist would evaluate the child. (3) Dentist would examine the child's teeth and make a recommendation if teeth had to be extracted for the surgery. (4) Doctor would approve or disapprove the surgery. Many of children were suffering from malaria and could not be screened. (5) Vital signs were given along with blood tests and operation was scheduled. During this 10 day period, the staff approved 157 for the operation and sadly had to turn away several hundred. The child cannot be operated on until after six months; and since they cannot nurse the milk had to be fed with a spoon. Other factors include vital signs and physicals along with blood tests.

With JoJo's recommendation I was fortunate to follow a three-year old boy through the screening-operation- and recovery stages. Whenever JoJo (plastic surgeon from Philippines) was operating on this little boy-it was a miracle watching his little cleft lip change to a normal lip. JoJo would sing "Amazing Grace" during the procedure and after completion would say "Amen". This particular doctor had been volunteering with Operation Smile since 1982 which was birthdate of this organization. During recovery, a cleft lip is not as painful as a cleft palate and the recovery nurses pay close attention to these children. (I met a super young nurse named Megan who took care of the patients as her own. Megan taught me so much about the care these children need after an operation.) A cleft lip heals much faster than a cleft palate and in two or three days these children are able to smile.

A sad story of a Mother who brought her baby to hospital and left him. Most of medical work was completed but the child had several serious burns that took longer to heal and would need hospital care and then placed in an orphanage unless a family member came forward. Leaving a note at the hospital the Mother stated she had HIV and knew her time was limited.

Back to the hospital guard with the "hat"! I always greeted the guard every morning and usually told him that I liked his hat. On the last day of our mission, I received a wrapped gift. I asked JoJo about receiving gifts and he said to open it! In the box was the hat of the hospital guard. JoJo laughed and said he wanted to know my intentions and the gift showed his interest. I asked JoJo to clear this matter but I learned one has to be careful being too friendly. Another blessing in my life of meeting the Operation Team and volunteering to be a part of a child's healing process in Africa.

With Operation Smile, they issue round trip plane tickets but return passage schedule is open thus giving an opportunity to tour. Operation Smile stresses the need to know the culture and represent the organization in a positive and friendly attitude.

Therefore, Megan and I decided to schedule a safari in Kenya reserving a fancy African tent on the river watching hippos each morning. Killing animals in Kenya is not permitted; therefore taking pictures is encouraged. Many poachers kill the elephants for the ivory and the babies are sent to a refuge for protection. We had a wonderful guide that was an expert of location of animals; and viewing all the wild animals from an open jeep was a thrill of a lifetime. (Zebras, cow buffalos, gazelles, giraffes, water buffalos, alligators, jackals, rhinos, lions, jackals, war hogs, hippos, baboons.) Thousands of pink flamingos on a lake was one of the prettiest sights. Our guide also planned a night tour which was an eye-opener of animals looking for food. Attending special musical dances that teach social patterns with colorful costumes to teach the values of work and maturity. The children attending were not bashful and many wanted to sit on our laps and harmonize with the African songs. Being on my own after Megan left, I reserved an African Straw Hut and listening to the baboons made me think of the children in Africa suffering from malaria and other diseases. Return trip to Nairobi to catch plane but took a detour to visit the home of film, "Out Of Africa" starring Robert Redford and Merle Streep. Leaving Africa but never forgetting the healing and good memories of this mission trip.

CHINA

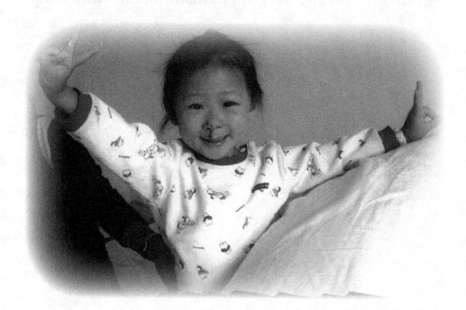

History of China and the Chinese culture is one of the oldest and greatest cultures in the world. The cultures along the Hwange He and Yangtze Rivers has grown into one of the world's most powerful and wealthy regions. It is the world's most populated country with a population of around 1,404 billion in 2017.

Operation Smile to Harbin,China : (knee how) Hello in Chinese. Originally a Manchu word meaning "a place for drying fishing nets" and also known as the "ice city" for its long and cold winters usually lasting from October to April. The long winter gives birth to the famous ice sculpturing events. Northeast Harbin lies near the Russian Border creating Russian architecture throughout the city. The strong Russian influence has once gained the nickname "Oriental Moscow". The strong Russian flavor continues to permeate the city today due to burgeoning trade and tourism between China and Russia. Over the years has been making full use of its geographical advantage and has played a major role in the advancement of China-Russian relations.

Settling in our hotel Sino-Swiss was appreciative of fresh fruit and flowers to welcome the Operation Team. The medical team consisted of fourteen from China, three from Philippines, one from Ireland, one from Russia, one from Singapore, one from Australia, one from Hong Kong, twenty eight from United States plus one from TEXAS. We were fortunate to have a group of medical students from China University. We screened 226 patients and surgeons operated on 129 children. The Chinese were very appreciated of Operation Smile and understood due to the screening process of their child not been selected.

If a picture is worth a thousand words-this picture of this little Chinese girl is worth a million words. She loved to "show off her new smile" and welcomes photographers.

Picture: This precious little boy was left in the streets to survive; but a very considerate lady found him and brought him to Operation Smile for a cleft lip. Joy of this story was the lady adopted him and now he has two reasons to smile.

The medical team of Operation Smile did a marvelous job for the Chinese and as they would say: xiexie/xiexie (Thank You-Thank you very much my friend.)

Since we are on our own after the mission with an open

flight return schedule; decided to visit one of the wonders if the world. It was an inspiring historical tour of the Great Walls of China. Had to use a trolley car to reach the top- but I did make a few stairs. Shopping in Beijing was a savings buying silk blouses and jade. Operation Smile always stated you are on your own with after the mission and finances and tours are your responsibility. Only problem I encountered was using the "squat pots" but if you have to go-you go. China was working on the Olympics of 2008 and were focusing on traffic problems and of course buying "toilets"!

Many blessings for China from the Operation Mission Team of 2005.

PHNOM PENH, CAMBODIA MISSION

(Sahbai/sahbai na) We are happy/very happy to welcome Operation Smile.

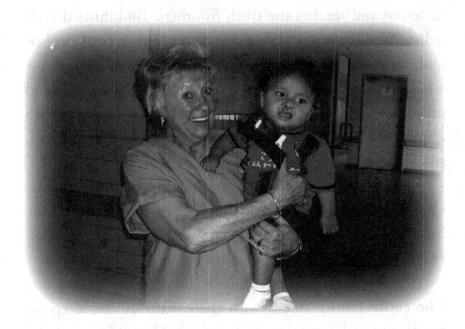

Cambodia is located in the southern part of the Indochina peninsula in Southeast Asia. Bordered by Thailand to North West, Laos to the North East, and Viet Nam to east. The population is 1529 million. Cambodia seems to have achieved a measure of tenuous stability. It still faces severe economic difficulties (international aid is helping with health care), political fighting, and dangers from unexploded bombs.

Phnom Penh (capital of Cambodia) was once known as "Pearl of Asia" because it was considered one of the loveliest French-built cities in Indochina. Royal Palace in Phnom Penh is a complex of buildings which serve as the royal residence of the King of Cambodia. Ninety-seven percent believe in Buddhism with the remaining three percent Islam, Christianity, and Tribal Animism. Buddha: "The Awaken One" is someone who has woken the truth of the mind and suffering and teaches the truth to others. Buddhists do not believe Buddha is a God, but that he is a human being woken and can see the true way the mind works. Tribal Animism is a belief that the world is a community of living persons and only some are human. Animism is a belief that all things have a spirit or soul including animals, plants, rivers, mountains, stars, the moon and sun.

Medical Team: One from Cambodia, Three from Canada, One from Brazil, One from China, Two from Hawaii, One from Venezuela, One from Singapore, Six from Philippines, twenty-six from United States and one ole Texan.

After the screening, schedules were made for the patients. The entire family comes with their bedrolls and sleep on the floor until operation is complete. The majority of the operations were cleft lip operations with a successful smile for the child.

The mission director suggested the student sponsor and students visit a home for the sexually abuse children to show our interest and passion for these children. The children were happy to see us and we entertained them the best we could singing songs and dancing to their music. "Happy" the puppet was a hit!

Another visit was to a large sewing building of young single pregnant girls. They were talented seamstresses earning their pay for the future ahead. Always smiling and congential.

The last tour was to the "killing fields of Cambodia" which is a number of sites scattered throughout Cambodia. The Klmer Rouge-Buddhist religion did not want anyone to be educated- so he had orders to kill anyone interested in education. It is estimated over 20,000 mass graves are located in Cambodia where an estimate of more than a million children and adults were killed and buried. (1975-1979) This tour broke our hearts Rouge Killing Fields.

SANTA CRUZ, BOLIVIA: SOUTH AMERICA

Nnenna (Welcome Operation Smile)

Bolivia is said to be one of the poorest countries in South America but the Andean landscapes and ancient civilizations made it a rich and exciting country. It is the highest altitude of the Latin American republics causing a problem with altitude sickness. It is also the most indigenous country on the continent, with more than 50% of population maintaining values and beliefs. The population of Bolivia is about 8.8 million with 30% Quechua Indian, 25% Mestizo, 30% Aymara Indian, and approximately 15% Spanish/European.

Santa Cruz is the largest city in Bolivia situated on the Pirai River in the eastern tropical lowlands. Seventy % of people live in the metropolitan areas with a population of 1.45 million. Main religions are Evangelical/Pentecost, Catholic, and Protestant. Santa Cruz has long been reputed to be a drug trafficking center but now it is enjoying an agriculture boom. Brave Gauchos are known for being expert horse riders with first class registered horses.

Fifty volunteers were on this mission consisting of plastic surgeon, doctors, nurses, educational specialists, dentist, speech therapist, and medical records. The volunteers were from Bolivia, Argentina, Canada, England, China and the United States including a Texan. Two hundred twenty six patients were screened and one-hundred thirty qualified for operations. Being a student sponsor, we bathed the children and dress them for surgery; but they selected their own gowns with excitement. Boys preferred bright colors and girls loved the pastel colors. (Must give credit to different organizations and churches in the United States who made the gowns combined with a traveling bag containing a stuff animal, washcloth, soap, toothpaste, and a comb.

After the mission, we visited a Quarter Horse Farm and one of the largest butterfly sanctuaries in Bolivia. Parrots are on every tree but one particular parrot was sitting alone. The Bolivians stated the female parrot had died and his male mate was grieving- usually until he died. We all enjoyed the replica of the Statue of Liberty in the center of the city which made us feel at home.

Bless the one hundred and thirty children who received 'SMILES' on this Operation Smile mission.

MAHUHAY

(welcome: Filipino greeting) Operation
Smile to Cebu, Philippines

T he Philippines, officially known as the Republic of the
Philippines, is an island country located in Southwest
Asia with Manila as its capital. The Philippines
comprise of 7,107 islands in the western Pacific Ocean. The

Philippines is the world's 12th most populous country with a population of 90 million people. Disasters of volcanoes and typhoons have caused many deaths in this island. The main religion is Roman Catholic but some of the small islands practice Islam. Oldest Catholic Church in the Philippines is located in Cebu. Interesting cuisine dishes are: Whole roasted pigs, oxtail and beef intestines baked in a peanut sauce, and pork or fish as a tamarind stew. Today, Philippines are a leader in manufacturing electronics and other high tech components. According to the 1987 Philippine Constitution, Filipino and English are the official languages. (History) In 1942 the islands fell under Japanese occupation during World War II, and US Forces and Filipinos fought together during 1944-1945 to regain control with General Douglas MacArthur as U.S. Commander. General MacArthur received the Medal of Honor for his service in the Philippines Campaign, which made him and his father, Arthur MacArthur Jr. first son and father to be awarded this medal. Franklin Roosevelt was president during this campaign and he admired General Douglas Macarthur famous quote, "Old Soldiers Never Die: They Just Fade Away".

The location of the mission was Cebu, Philippines with a population of 2.94 million and a maximum amount of cell phones. Cebu has been known as the Queen City of the South with the first established indigenous settlement in the West Philippines. Sixty volunteers (plastic surgeons, anesthesiologists, pediatricians, dentist, nurses, speech therapists, electronic medical record coordinator, student sponsor, child specialist, high school students and a mission coordinator with the majority of staff from the Philippines.

Over 500 children were screened and 230 operations were completed in 6 days using 6 operating tables. Each child did receive a complete physical from attending doctors and nurses; the children that were not accepted for this mission will be posted on a waiting list for the next year. The citizens were patient and thankful for helping their children.

The students and I visited St. Martin De Porres Special School for mentally challenged and hearing-impaired children. The range of "Special Needs" includes those with: Hearing Impairment, Cerebral Palsy, Down Syndrome, Autism, and other Learning Difficulties. The students danced with them, sang songs, and hugs were given and of course "Happy" the puppet was the main star.

Leaving this beautiful country of friendly people with new smiles, I remembered the saying from St. Martin School: "For our children…..Their happiness first, all else follows."

Off to Australia to represent Operation Smile: Aussie country with a greeting of G'day Mate ! Australia "southern legend of unknown land" is comprised of 6 states: New South Wales, Queensland, South Australia, Tasmania, Victoria, and Western Australia. This continent has 2,941,300 square miles and is surrounded by the Indian and Pacific Oceans with 21,262 miles of coastline with a population of 24.64 million.

Great Barrier Reef dates back to the last Ice Age when the current Continental Shelf was exposed. When the sea level rose, all the beaches, dunes, and barrier islands were submerged, providing the perfect platform for reef colonies which is the tiny organisms that build coral. As the sea level rose, the reef grew more. In periods when the level failed, exposed coral broke off and this reef debris raised the level of the shelf floor in the reef zone, enabling more reef to be built. It is the world's largest coral reef and extends over 1,240 miles with every type of fish imaginable Today, the Great Barrier Reef is home to about 350 species of coral, about 10,000 species of sponges, more than 4,000 species of Mollusca, about 150 species of echinoderms and more than 1500 species of fish. Many of us remember Steve Irvin of Australia also known as the "Crocodile Hunter", zoo keeper, television personality, and wildlife expert. He died in 2006 after been pierced in the chest by a stingray while filming in the Great Barrier Reef for an underwater document. His wife, (Terri), daughter,(Bindi) and son (Robert) continue his legacy at the Australian zoo.

The largest part of Australia is desert or known as the outback country. This country has the greatest number of reptiles (fresh water and salt water) with 755 different species. Marsupials consist of kangaroos, koala, and wombats. Most popular birds are the emus and kookaburra.

Queen Elizabeth is recognized as the queen but the government power is represented by the Governor-General and Prime Minister. Monarch of Australia. English is the national language and Australia is ranked #8 in the world of education. School of the Air broadcasts lessons Via Radio signals to pupils living in remote areas. Australian schools are among the finest in the world with small classes, individual teaching, University trained, and advanced technology. Visiting an International School and understanding their curriculum for these young students as far as their career future was an inspiration for any educator. The children's hospitals are known for their caring and friendly staff in Australia. .

Tour to a Coffee plantation was interesting; Journey on the Freshwater Railway traveling from cane fields of Cairns to the tropical rainforest of Kuranda was breath-taking; Cairns Tropical Zoo interacting with the animals, free flight bird show including the majestic Sea Eagles, native and exotic snakes and lizards, kangaroos, and holding a Koala was entertaining. BUT swimming in the Barrier Reef with a fourteen year old super swimmer guide (Bob) was challenging and best way to end a tour of "Aussie Country". Teaching this Granny to snorkel was a demanding job for this young chap and stated he would not leave my side. The water was warm and relatively safe and being a part of the amazing underwater world was beyond description with all the types of coral. The whole underwater landscape is different. Fish change color, parrot fish sleep in a sack made from their own saliva. Bottom-scuttlers come out to feed and mysterious eyes watch you constantly. Bob held my hand whenever a very large turtle passed us. I am so thankful for young people that care about others, Thank you, Bob.

I loved this country—next to TEXAS. People are friendly and the kangaroos are even friendlier. Must say I was leery of the crocodiles at the Carnes Zoo along with the Python Snakes.

"Cherrio" to my friends "Down yonder"!

OPERATION SMILE TO: CHINANDEGA, NICARAGUA

Nicaragua is a small country in the Central American Isthmus. The multi-ethnic of indigenous, European, and Asian heritage embarks the population of about six million people mostly of Mestizos which is mixed European and Indian Ancestry. Spanish is the common language and mainly Catholic religion. Indigenous tribes on the Mesquito Coast speak their own language. The location of "Masaya Volcano" has been called the "Gates of Hell" because of the many earthquakes in this country. San Cristobal Volcano, also known as Elviejo is the highest and one of the most active volcanoes in Nicaragua. In 1998 "Hurricane Mitch" killed more than 1800 Nicaraguans which was the second deadlist Atlantic hurricane on record.

"Hola" (hello) Chinandega: The operation smile team traveled by bus to this city after air travel from the capital city of Managua. We passed a monument erected to remember 1000 people killed in 1992 mudslide and our hearts felt the pain.

Upon arrival we knew this was a very poor country with economic problems but the citizens were friendly and appreciative. The mission team screened over 300 patients and provided 214 surgical procedures. As student sponsor, my students presented a program to an orphanage and talked to a blind school about health and cleanliness. An unusual pet was living at the hospital "a chicken" and we laughed every morning strutting around like he owned the place. Another unusual guest was a young 16 yr. old boy raised by the hospital and occupied his own room at the hospital after been left as a baby by unknown parents. Oh! Did he make acquaintances with everyone on the mission team. Another surprise was Donald and Vanessa Trump visiting and helping with the children with a friendly attitude and thanking everyone. Must give credit to a popular sport of baseball; Texas Ranger Pitcher Vicente Padilla was the first baseball player from Nicaragua to play in the Major League and in 1991 became the first Latin-born pitcher to throw a perfect game against the Dodgers. Boxing is the second most popular sport in Nicaragua.

Nicaragua may be a poor country but their heart is made of gold.

Operation Smile encourages the volunteers to continue touring after the mission to help close the borders with a peaceful attitude.

A relaxing vacation in Costa Rica after long hours with hospital was "what the doctor ordered". Costa Rica's coffee plantations, sugar cane fields, rainforest, waterfalls, forest critters, tropical birds, funny monkeys, ugly snakes, colorful butterflies, strange frogs, and numerous hummingbirds were God's creatures; but the expense of this country was a total shock. The beauty was worth every last dollar!

A tour to the Panama Canal completed the adventure to Central America and is truly one of the great wonders of the world. In 1904 United States purchased the rights of the canal for $40 million from the French. It took 10 years of labor of more than 75,000 men and women and almost $400 million to complete the work on the canal. The SS Ancon made the first official ocean-to-ocean through the waterway on August 15, 1914.The highest toll for transiting the Canal was paid by TEXAS carrying 65,299 tons of oil and holds the record; the lowest toll for transiting the Canal was paid by Richard Halliburton, who paid 36 cents to swim across the canal from August 14 to August 23, 1928. President Carter signed an international treaty to give the Canal to Panama in 1977 and a neutrality treaty was signed for times of peace and war. Since release to Panama, the canal in seven years has made $2.3 billion to the State of Panama.

The canal is 50 miles from Atlantic to Pacific and requires 8 to 10 hours for an average ship to transit the canal. Using a system of locks with chambers of gates that open and close for the transit of the ships. The locks operate as water elevators that raise the ship from sea level to the Gatlin Lake in their transit of the channel. Each lock chamber is 110 feet wide and 1000 feet long. The canal total watershed output will augment more than 300 million gallons of water per day. Watching 10 ships pass through the canal was an engineer dream.

"Voypa' I Chanti"—Panama words for " I'm going home" but carrying your history with me.

OPERATION SMILE (2007)

ANMAN, JORDAN

The Middle East kingdom of Jordan is bordered on the West by Israel and the Dead Sea, on the North by Syria, on the East by Iraq, and on the South by Saudi Arabia. Arid hills and mountains make up most of the country. The southern section of the Jordan River flows through the country. The population of Jordan in 2007 was estimated at 6,053,193 and Amman which is the capital is estimated at 2,677, 500. The official language is Arabic and English; Ethnic/race is 98% Arab; and religions 94% Muslim, 6 % Christian and Greek Orthodox. In 1999, former King Hussein deposed his brother, Prince Hassan, who had been heir apparent for 34 years, and named his eldest son as the new crown prince. A month later, King Hussein died of cancer, and Abdullah, 37, a popular military leader became king. HISTORY: Jordan's stance during the Persian War strained relations with the United States and led to the termination of U.S. aid. In 1991, the signing of a national charter meaning political parties were permitted in exchange for acceptance of constitution; and the monarchy and Middle East peace talks helped restore the country's relations with the United States. First bombings of three suicide bombings by Iraqis blasted hotels in Amman killing 57 people and wounding 115. The terrorist group, al-Qaeda in Iraq, claimed responsibility, contending Jordan had been targeted because of its friendly relations with the United States. (Sadly the bombings continues)

Amman, the modern and ancient capital of Jordan, is one of the oldest continuously inhabited in the world. The city's modern buildings blend with the remnants of ancient civilizations. Recent excavations have uncovered homes and towers believed to have been built during the Age with many references to the Bible. Amman was known in the Old Testament as "City of Waters".

Since Operation Smile was working with volunteers from Jordan, it was necessary to respect their religion. Sumni-Islam is the dominant religion in Jordan with Muslims make-up about 93% of the country's population. Religious language of Muslims is their Holy Book called Quran or Koran. Salat which is the most important obligations of Islam faith praying and bowing down to Allah in prayer five times each day. Beliefs of Islam teach about Allah (God), prophets, Books of revelation, angels, heaven and hell, destiny, free will, and creation of the earth. Five pillars of faith: (1) Hajj: Pilgrimage to Holy City of Mecca once a year. (2) Sawm: Ritual fasting. (3) Shahadah: Faith. (4) Salat: Daily prayers. (5) Give to charity and aiding the poor. Praying any quiet place, office, home, or Mosques and missing prayer is considered a serious lapse of faith for devout Muslims.

Jordan Mission (2007): Operation Smile celebrated their twenty-fifth Anniversary as "World Journey of Smiles" in twenty five countries. Free examinations were given to 7,320 patients; 4,149 surgeries were performed on children born with cleft lips and cleft palates. More than 1,700 volunteers from 44 countries made these missions possible for the 25th anniversary of Operation Smile. (1982-2007) World Journey of Smiles began in the Philippines, in the same hospital co-founders Dr. Bill Magee and Kathy Magee led the first mission after fund-raising for the costs in Operation Smile's hometown of Norfolk, Virginia. In 25 years Operation Smile has treated more than 175,000 children. (Today : 2019 the surgeries and volunteers have more than double; and of course the missions have increased more than double in developing countries. The 50th anniversary in 2032 will be overwhelming operating on the children of the world) Operation Smile brings nations and people of the world closer together through the sharing of medical expertise, volunteers, training, resources, and passion for changing children's lives.

Operation Smile screened 426 children in Jordan (2007) and in nine days the doctors operated on 116 and 42 Iraq children. (Operation Smile charted a plane to fly the Iraq children to Jordan.) Besides palates and lips there were also facial deformities and burns due to the war in Iraq. An interview with a 16 yr. young Iraq man who brought his 9 yr. brother for a cleft lip operation was depressing but admiration for this young man. Their Father had been killed by a terrorist who chopped off his head and his Mother was suffering mentally. This well-mannered young man quit school to take care of his 11 siblings. The Iraq guardians and children were patient and courteous waiting 4-5 hours to be screened.

This mission consisted of 42 from Jordan and we honored their prayer time. Also, 2 from Canada, 3 from Italy, and 21 from U.S. with 2 TEXANS volunteered for this Operation Smile Mission. It was recommended by the mission chairman to tour Petra, Jordan since Petra is the treasure of the ancient world, hidden behind an almost impenetrable barrier of rugged mountains. Riding camels through the rose-carved city made it even more mysterious. The Petra basin boasts over 800 individual monuments, buildings, tombs, baths, temples, arched gateways, and colonnaded streets that were mostly carved from sandstone. It has been said, "there is nothing in the world that resembles it" and now it is a world heritage site being one of the 7 Wonders of the World.

Being a student sponsor, two Mormon girls from Utah were assigned to me and as usual the students surpassed their responsibilities for being perfect role models for these children. Duties of the students were to help with the screening process; help with bathing, give each child a "smiley bag" with gown, personal hygiene supplies with a stuff toy to hug; and made sure they would have a smooth transition to operating room through child play. Sometimes it would be necessary to be with child in operating room but the students were always available in recovery room. When the children were released, a checklist of medical supplies and making sure the guardians understood all orders from doctors and nurses. We completed field trips with different programs to Modern Montession School (higher education) for children; SOS Children's Village Association caring for orphaned and abandoned children; Mental Hospital for Children; and a Refuge Center. The refuge center had a very small library and the same books were read several times. Whenever we presented our program, they listened eagerly and learned some English songs. A young 12yr.old boy sang us a song in Hebrew…beautiful voice and even we did not know the translation-but we knew the lyrics of a young boy who wanted to return to his homeland. These children open your eyes to be more appreciative of the opportunities we have in America.

Mission trip ending but a spiritual trip to Holy Lands with two precious Mormon students with parents' permission and one Presbyterian learned about religions and culture of Israel. Mormons believe first that Jesus Christ is their Savior and Redeemer. Their church's mission is to help or meet the challenges of this life so that one will be worthy of spiritual blessings of God. They strongly believe in service to others because Jesus spent his life serving others; and following his example brings happiness. (personal history from the girls) We were three people on a mission to learn about Jesus in the Holy Lands. An Operation Smile doctor recommended we stay at the Cathedral Church of St. George in Jerusalem. A feeling of safety with nice rooms and reasonable charge with payment given to the Church. The Priests requested us to participate in prayers, songs, and attend communion in the early mornings which enlightened our tour in Jerusalem. Besides giving us a feeling of peace and gratitude, they offered historical suggestions for our stay in this Holy City to begin with the birthplace of Jesus in Bethlehem. Visiting the site of the Last Supper when Jesus sat down for his last meal with his twelve disciples; and stated one of them would betray him. Jesus prayed in the Garden of Gethsemane: Luke 22:42-44 "Father, if is Your will, take this cup away from Me; nevertheless not My will, but Yours, be done. Then an angel appeared to Him from heaven, strengthening Him. And being in agony. He prayed more earnestly. Then His sweat became like great drops of blood falling down to the ground. (THE HOLY BIBLE. The New King James Version: Thomas Nelson Publishers.). Luke 22: 47-48 And while He was speaking, "behold a multitude; and he who was called "Judas, one of the twelve, went before them and drew near to Jesus to kiss him. But Jesus said to him. Judas are you betraying the Son of Man with a kiss?" .THE HOLY BIBLE NEW KING JAMES VERSION: Thomas Nelson Publishers. The Garden today is well manicured and peaceful feeling the spirit of Jesus. Walking the steps of Jesus before the crucifixion called the Via Dolorosa with fourteen stations was painful for us. The Holy Sepulcher or Church of Resurrection in the old city of Jerusalem is the location where Jesus was crucified. The Mount of Olives is a Jewish cemetery and a place for Christian worship. We dressed according to Jewish belief praying at the West Wall or the Wailing Wall and entering the tomb of Jesus. The girls swimming in the Dead Sea (salt water) was an unforgettable sight using the mud to cleanse themselves. Too many spiritual adventures to list; and as the girls waved good-by boarding the plane to go home, I will always have a special place in my heart for these "two sweet Mormon girls".

Jesus will always love the children of the world. I only hope this non-fiction book <u>Fading Memories</u> has enlightened our views concerning the importance of nurturing children. History-geography-personal experiences-ancestors-descendants play an important part of the life of a child. CHILDREN BUILD BRIDGES OF PEACE THROUGHOUT THE WORLD.

Psalms 127:3 Behold, Children are a heritage from the Lord, the fruit of the womb is a reward.